GRAPHIC EXCELLENCE

GRAPHIC EXCELLENCE

By the Editors of *Studio Magazine*

PBC INTERNATIONAL, INC. ● New York

BOOK DESIGN BY ROGER E. MURRAY, STUDIO MAGAZINE

Distributor to the book trade in the United States:
Rizzoli International Publications, Inc.
597 Fifth Avenue
New York, NY 10017

Distributor to the art trade in the United States:
Letraset USA
40 Eisenhower Drive
Paramus, NJ 07653

Distributor in Canada:
Letraset Canada Limited
555 Alden Road
Markham, Ontario L3R 3L5, Canada

Distributed throughout the rest of the world by:
Hearst Books International
105 Madison Avenue
New York, NY 10016

Copyright © 1987 by The Studio Magazine and PBC International, Inc. All rights reserved. No part of this book may be reproduced in any form whatsoever without written permission of the copyright owner, PBC International, Inc., One School Street, Glen Cove, NY 11542.

ISBN 0-86636-071-9

Library of Congress Catalog Card Number 87-061203

Printed in Hong Kong
10 9 8 7 6 5 4 3 2

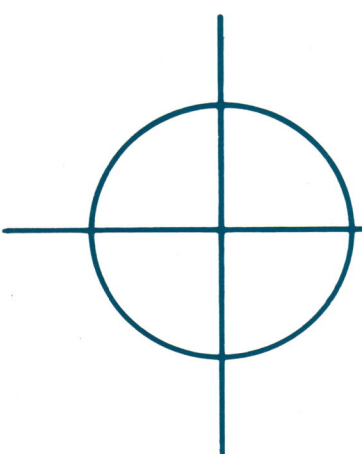

Contents

Introduction 8

The Judges of GRAPHIC EXCELLENCE 10

CHAPTER 1
Art Direction 12
Art direction as "the art of creatively choreographing the various elements necessary to make up practically any form of visual and/or written communication"

CHAPTER 2
Graphic Design 42
Diverse media, type styles and composition in logos, brochures, annual reports and more

CHAPTER 3
Photography 68
Variety and creativity in a wide range of subject matter and photographic styles

CHAPTER **4**
Illustration 94
Illustrations which are witty, whimsical, and frightening, in media ranging from watercolor and airbrush to poster paint

CHAPTER **5**
Printing 128
Technical excellence in a field where technology has altered and improved performance dramatically

CHAPTER **6**
Typography 152
Type used as design in brochures, advertisements, posters, stationery and more

CHAPTER **7**
Copywriting 164
Compelling copywriting in consumer advertisements, brochures, outdoor advertising and other categories

Appendix 186
A directory of names and addresses lists art directors, graphic designers, photographers, illustrators, printers, typographers, and copywriters.

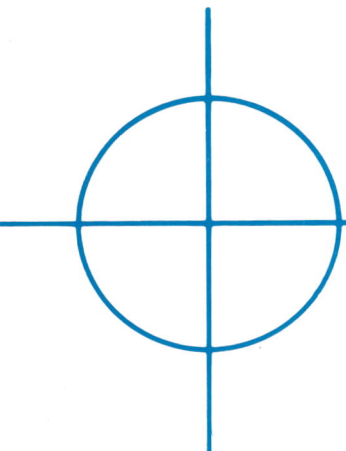

INTRODUCTION

In a world of advancing electronic technology, it is encouraging to see the creative mind of the artist bringing form, color, and content to our culture, and often with the simplest tools.

The essence of good art direction can be stated with just a pencil sketch. Likewise, the copywriter needs only pen and paper to communicate an idea. The designer can use a few markers and a pad to share his creative thoughts and the photographer can utilize a basic camera outfit to produce an image of a different slant.

Much of this will change over the next 10 years as art directors, graphic designers, copywriters, photographers, typesetters, illustrators and printers implement computer technology in an effort to remain competitive and innovative.

This book, however, looks back over the last 10 years – a period relatively untouched by such foreign phrases as 'desktop publishing' and 'photographic art direction by video'.

It was a significant era for the professional creative community as they moved away from a very distinctive sixties style into the unknown seventies. Creatively speaking it was a slow start to a new decade and only in the late seventies to early eighties did we see new trends emerging. The award-winning works presented here reflect the creative move away from a 'standard' look to an individualistic style. Some trends are evident, though, such as condensed, spaced-out type in the graphic design category, and a bold graphic approach to some of the photography in the photographic category.

This eclectic showcase is a presentation of the award-winning pieces that were chosen from 3,500 entries in '76-86 The Creative Decade' – an international graphic arts competition created and sponsored by Studio Magazine.

The readers of this professional graphic arts publication were invited to enter their best work from this 10-year period. Naturally, the majority of the entrants chose to submit their most recent projects, but it is interesting to note that many award-winning pieces have a timeless quality and do not fall into a specific trend or dated era.

A directory of award-winners is included to allow you the opportunity to directly contact these outstanding creators for project development or consultation.

Studio Magazine offers its readers in 25 countries the chance to participate in a similar prestigious awards program each year. The seven categories of this particular program – Art Direction, Graphic Design, Photography, Illustration, Typography, Printing, and Copywriting, are represented here in order of the judges' choice – Gold, Silver and Merit awards, and the number of awards given at each of these three levels was determined solely by the judges.

Roger E. Murray
Publisher/Creative Director
Studio Magazine

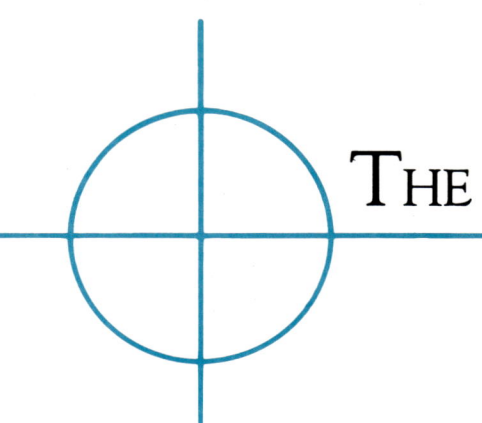

The Judges of Graphic Excellence

Mike Tott

Vice President and Senior Art Director at J. Walter Thompson in Montreal, Mike Tott has experienced many sides of design and advertising art. Mr. Tott spent three years working in art studios before moving on to advertising agencies. He has worked on such varied accounts as Players Cigarettes, Kraft Foods, Pepsi-Cola, Clear Eyes and Laura Ashley. A winner of numerous national and international awards, Mike Tott holds a fine reputation within the industry. Born in England he currently resides in Montreal with his wife and two young children.

"...the person with the most talent does not necessarily win – it's the person with a little talent who really pushes himself the hardest."
MIKE TOTT

Michael Maynard

Michael Maynard, a teacher of graphic design at Georgian College, has worked as a production manager for a weekly Boston newspaper, as art director of news graphics for WCVB-TV, Boston, and as a designer with TVOntario. Mr. Maynard has received design awards for projects with the public and private sector in the U.S. and Canada; is Vice-President of the Society of Graphic Designers of Canada, (Ontario Chapter), and is a member of the Toronto Art Directors Club and AIGA.

"We tried to select pieces that reflect a viewpoint – reflect the individual who created it, and was singularly quite distinctive and unique"
MICHAEL MAYNARD

Steve Pigeon

Steve Pigeon is President and General Manager of Masterfile Stock Photo Library. Internationally recognized as one of Canada's leading authorities on stock photography, Mr. Pigeon has been instrumental in developing the Canadian stock photo market for the advertising and graphics industry in Canada. Mr. Pigeon managed the Image Bank of Canada from 1975 to 1983, forming Masterfile in 1981. Born in Montreal, he now resides in Toronto with his wife and two sons.

"All the judges were very fair and open-minded – there were no mad, nationalistic flagwavers amongst us."
STEVE PIGEON

Duncan McGregor

Duncan McGregor is President of Arthurs-Jones Lithographing Limited and has spent more than twenty-two years in the graphic arts industry. His experience ranges from stripping and platemaking to bindery and printing. Mr. McGregor and a former partner purchased Arthurs-Jones in 1976.

"It takes a large number of elements working together to make (a printed piece) Gold."
DUNCAN McGREGOR

Paula Scher

Paula Scher is a founding partner in Koppel & Scher. Ms. Scher has authored and designed two books, and has had numerous articles on design practice and theory appear in *Print Magazine*, *Ad Week* and the *AIGA Journal*. Her designs have been collected by a number of Museums including the Museum of Modern Art and the Beauborg Museum (Paris). She has won many awards from various societies and magazines, including 4 Grammy nominations for Cover of the Year from the National Association for Recording Arts and Sciences.

"What were we looking for? Idea. Design. A combination of both." — PAULA SCHER

Seymour Chwast

Seymour Chwast is a founding partner of The Pushpin Group, of which he is the director, and was honoured at the Louvre in Paris in a two-month retrospective exhibition entitled 'The Push Pin Style'. The recipient of a number of medals and awards, Mr. Chwast was voted into the Art Directors Hall of Fame and his posters are in the permanent collection of New York's Museum of Modern Art, as well as the Cooper-Hewitt Museum of the Smithsonian Institution, the Library of Congress and the Gutenberg Museum.

"We were looking for clarity of idea, information and craft. The way it is put together." — SEYMOUR CHWAST

Ursula Kaiser

Art Director of *Your Money Magazine*, Ursula Kaiser is the past president of the Art Directors Club of Toronto. A two-time gold award winner from the National Magazines Foundation, Ms. Kaiser currently resides on the Board of Directors for both the Art Directors Club of Toronto and the National Magazine Awards Foundation. Ms. Kaiser has worked as an art director since 1973 for such various publications as *Fugue Magazine*, *Quest*, *City Woman*, *Homemakers/Madame au Foyer*, and *The Toronto Star* and has also art directed for a number of advertising agencies.

'We were looking for pieces that achieved a high standard in concept, design and execution." — URSULA KAISER

Raymond Lee

Raymond Lee is President and Creative Director of Raymond Lee & Associates Ltd. Mr. Lee has won over 200 awards for creative achievements, including the Andy Award in New York, the NYAD Award, Art Directors Club Award, Marketing Award and the Clio International. His work has appeared in a number of publications and magazines. He is a member of the American Institute of Graphic Arts and the Institute of Canadian Advertising and a past director of both the Canadian Institute of Advertising and the Society of Ont. Advertisers and past Vice President of the Art Directors Club of Toronto.

"...creative people need encouragement. Our job is not creating pure art – it is creating marketing communications." — RAYMOND LEE

CHAPTER 1
GRAPHIC EXCELLENCE

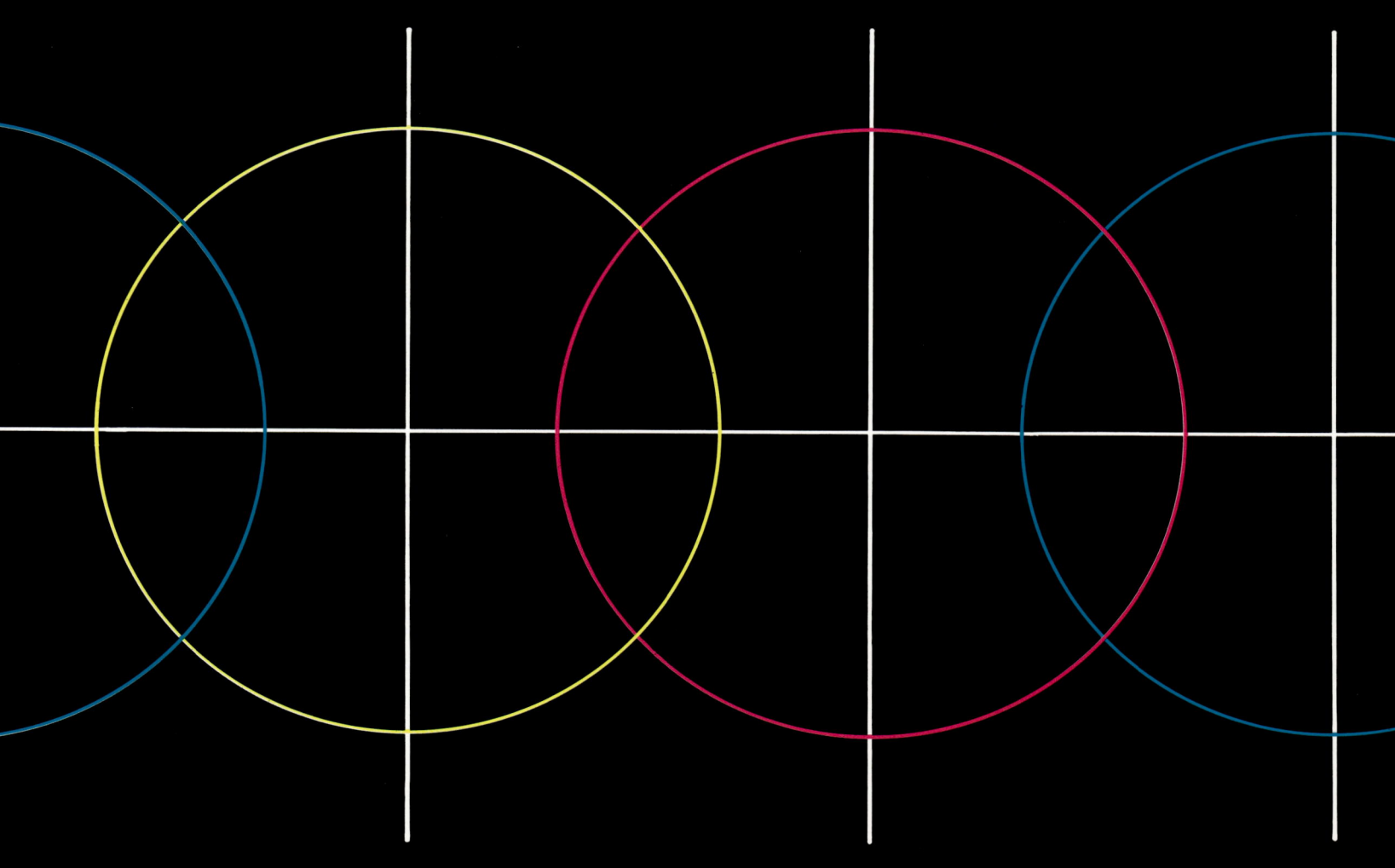

ART DIRECTION

This category can be defined as "the art of creatively choreographing the various elements necessary to make up practically any form of visual and/or written communication, whether for advertising, editorial, or promotional."

Among winning designations for art direction are consumer magazine ad, outdoor transit ad, advertising poster and advertising photography, trade publication ad, newspaper advertisement, annual report, and advertising illustration.

This chapter serves as a showcase for creativity and excellence in advertising, and gives credit to the people who coordinate all the elements which make a creative project worthy of praise.

GOLD

ART DIRECTION

Happily, financial freedom is not the exclusive right of the wealthy.

Midland Doherty

Financial freedom need not be narrowly defined as castles in Spain. Polo on weekends. And St. Moritz in the winter.

To many, financial freedom means being able to provide a challenging education and a stimulating environment for their children to grow in. Financial freedom means having the money and the time to pursue an area of interest for the pure joy of it. Surely it also means retiring when you want to, not when you have to. It is retirement with dignity and optimism.

Now, of all the financial advisors available to assist those who seek financial freedom, you will find no company more appropriate or sympathetic to these goals than Midland Doherty.

Since its founding, Midland Doherty has held that the joyous thing about attaining financial freedom is that it invariably leads to other freedoms. The freedom of choice and mobility. As well as freedom from fear and anxiety. If upon reflection these thoughts seem harmonious to you, then let us join forces. In search of financial freedom.

In search of financial freedom.

The day you retire should be as full of anticipation as the last day of school.

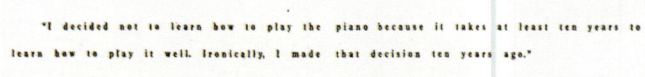

CONSUMER MAGAZINE AD - SERIES

AWARDED TO
 Allan Kazmer / Steve Thursby
CREATIVE DIRECTOR
 Allan Kazmer
ART DIRECTOR
 Steve Thursby
PHOTOGRAPHERS
 Nigel Dickson / Bert Bell
TYPOGRAPHER / WRITER
 Typsettra Ltd. / Allan Kazmer
ADVERTISING AGENCY
 Doyle Dane Bernbach Advertising Ltd.
CLIENT
 Midland Doherty Ltd.

14 GRAPHIC EXCELLENCE

SILVER

ART DIRECTION

CONSUMER MAGAZINE AD - SERIES
AWARDED TO
  Leon Berger / Dave Bouquet
  Paul Lavoie / Ron Caplan
  J. Walter Thompson - Montreal
CREATIVE DIRECTOR
  Leon Berger
ART DIRECTORS
  Paul Lavoie / Dave Bouquet
PHOTOGRAPHER
  Michel Pilon
WRITER
  Ron Caplan
ADVERTISING AGENCY
  J. Walter Thompson - Montreal
CLIENT
  Smith & Nephew

ART DIRECTION 15

SILVER
ART DIRECTION

OUTDOOR TRANSIT AD - SERIES
AWARDED TO
  Scali, McCabe, Sloves (Canada) Ltd.
CREATIVE DIRECTOR
  Gary E. Prouk
ART DIRECTOR
  Andre Morkel
PHOTOGRAPHERS
  Richard Sharabura / Nigel Dickson
  Photo Researchers
WRITER
  Gary E. Prouk
ILLUSTRATORS
  Bill Payne / Bob Fortier
  Ted Michener / David Phillips
ADVERTISING AGENCY
  Scali, McCabe, Sloves (Canada) Ltd.
CLIENT
  Cadbury Schweppes Canada

SILVER

ART DIRECTION

CONSUMER MAGAZINE AD
AWARDED TO
 Leon Berger / Terry Tomalty
 J. Walter Thompson - Montreal
CREATIVE DIRECTOR
 Leon Berger
ART DIRECTOR
 Terry Tomalty
PHOTOGRAPHER
 Larry Williams
WRITER
 Leon Berger
ADVERTISING AGENCY
 J. Walter Thompson - Montreal
CLIENT
 Kraft Limited

OUTDOOR TRANSIT AD
AWARDED TO
 Scali, McCabe, Sloves (Canada) Ltd.
CREATIVE DIRECTOR
 Gary E. Prouk
ART DIRECTOR
 Tony Kerr
PHOTOGRAPHER
 Olga Tracey
TYPOGRAPHER
 Typsettra Ltd.
WRITER
 Brian Quennell
ADVERTISING AGENCY
 Scali, McCabe, Sloves (Canada) Ltd.
CLIENT
 Apple Canada Inc.

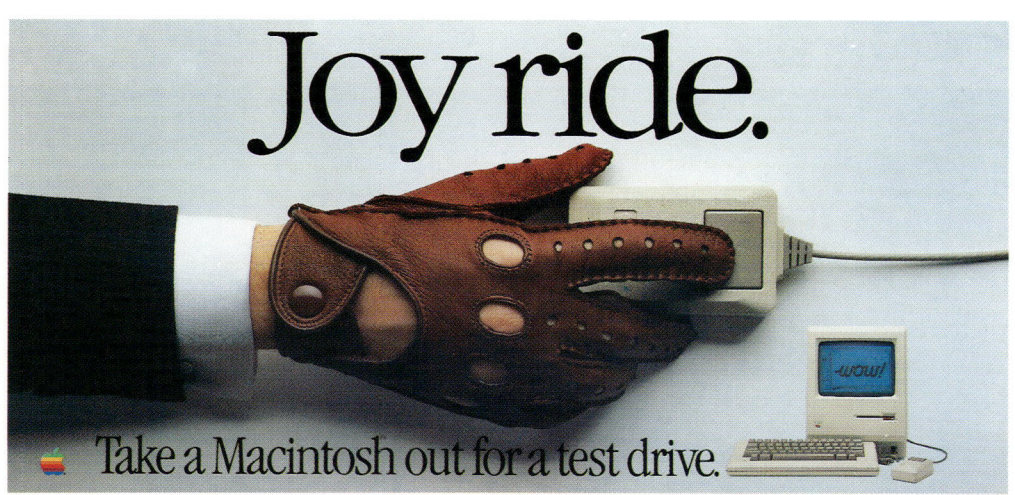

ART DIRECTION 17

SILVER
ART DIRECTION

355ml in the shade.

ADVERTISING POSTER

AWARDED TO
  Allan Kazmer / Steve Thursby
CREATIVE DIRECTOR / WRITER
  Allan Kazmer
ART DIRECTOR / WRITER
  Steve Thursby
ILLUSTRATOR
  Roger Hill
TYPOGRAPHER
  Typsettra Ltd.
PRODUCTION SUPERVISOR
  John Stevenson
ADVERTISING AGENCY
  Doyle Dane Bernbach Advertising Ltd.
CLIENT
  Heineken Marketing Canada

ADVERTISING PHOTOGRAPHY

AWARDED TO
  Jim Burt
CREATIVE DIRECTOR
  Graham Watt
ART DIRECTOR / DESIGNER
  Jim Burt
PHOTOGRAPHER
  Ivor Sharp
MODEL
  Harriet England
WRITER
  Graham Watt
ADVERTISING AGENCY
  McKim/Watt Burt
CLIENT
  Ontario Milk Marketing Board

SILVER

ART DIRECTION

TRADE PUBLICATION AD

AWARDED TO
  J. Walter Thompson Company Ltd.
CREATIVE DIRECTOR
  Bob Neighbour
ART DIRECTOR / DESIGNER
  Peter Jones
PHOTOGRAPHER
  Nigel Dickson
WRITER
  Hans Olaf Ein
ADVERTISING AGENCY
  J. Walter Thompson Company Ltd.
CLIENT
  Goodyear Canada Inc.
YEAR OF PRODUCTION 1982

OUTDOOR TRANSIT AD

AWARDED TO:
  Grant Tandy Ltd.
CREATIVE DIRECTOR
  David Adams
ART DIRECTOR
  Kieran McAuliffe
ILLUSTRATOR
  Thierry Thompson
ADVERTISING AGENCY
  Grant Tandy Ltd.
YEAR OF PRODUCTION 1985

ART DIRECTION 19

MERIT
ART DIRECTION

Love story.

CONSUMER MAGAZINE AD

AWARDED TO
 J. Walter Thompson Company Ltd.
CREATIVE DIRECTOR / WRITER
 Marlene Hore
ART DIRECTOR / DESIGNER
 Terry Tomalty
TYPOGRAPHER
 M & H Typography
COLOUR SEPARATOR
 Stanmont
ADVERTISING AGENCY
 J. Walter Thompson Company Ltd.
CLIENT
 Kraft Limited

CONSUMER MAGAZINE AD

AWARDED TO
 Allan Kazmer / Steve Thursby
CREATIVE DIRECTOR / WRITER
 Allan Kazmer
ART DIRECTOR
 Steve Thursby
PHOTOGRAPHER
 Ian Campbell
TYPOGRAPHER
 Typsettra Ltd.
ADVERTISING AGENCY
 Doyle Dane Bernbach Advertising Ltd.
CLIENT
 Heineken Marketing Canada

S   M   L   XL

20 GRAPHIC EXCELLENCE

MERIT

ART DIRECTION

The Porsche 911 owner: Some insights. There has been some conjecture over the years about the kinds of individuals who own the Porsche 911. Rather than provide answers, such conjecture generally raises more questions.

Is it true, for example, that 911 owners share a communion with their automobiles that goes beyond man's usual relationship with a machine?

And is it the case that 911 owners seek out the more tortuous roads, when they could travel a perfectly good highway? And would they understand the question?

They are sometimes asked, "Do you really need a Porsche?" The answer, of course, is no. Needs can be reduced to food, shelter and fire. So much for needs.

And, is there any credence to the notion that 911 owners recognize one another, as if they wore on their cheekbone a faint Porsche marque, visible only to the initiated? And so on.

Well as we have said, it is all conjecture, and will likely have to remain so.

Unless, of course, you should happen to be one of them.

For information on the 911, send your business card to Porsche Marketing Director, 1940 Eglinton Avenue East, Scarborough, Ontario M1L 2M2.

CONSUMER MAGAZINE AD - SERIES
AWARDED TO
  Viv Tate / Steve Thursby
CREATIVE DIRECTOR
  Allan Kazmer
ART DIRECTOR
  Steve Thursby
PHOTOGRAPHERS
  Terry Collier (Top)
  Terry Collier (Middle)
  Yuri Dojc (Bottom)
TYPOGRAPHER
  Typsettra Ltd.
WRITER
  Viv Tate
PRODUCTION SUPERVISOR
  John Stevenson
ADVERTISING AGENCY
  Doyle Dane Bernbach Advertising Ltd.
CLIENT
  Volkswagen Canada Inc.

When choosing a luxury automobile, remember: You didn't get where you are by running with the pack. Most luxury cars we see today seem to have been designed to reflect some stereotyped perception of the people who would drive them, as if such people required, like protective colouration, the security of a conventionally designed automobile.

At Porsche, we hold a different view of luxury cars. And of the people who drive them.

We recognize, for example, that a luxury automobile does not always have the luxury of ideal driving conditions. That the road ahead, as in life itself, is likely to turn up some unpleasant surprises.

The Porsche 928S is made for such moments. Its behaviour, even in the most arduous situations, is impeccable.

We also recognize that among those who drive luxury cars, there are individuals who, while they may feel at home in a grey suit, have no desire to drive a grey car, whatever its colour.

There is nothing 'grey' about the Porsche 928S. Its design is unique. Its luxury appointments are unlike anything you have ever experienced. It is totally apart from the pack.

And in this last regard, it is not unlike the individuals who come to own it.

For information on the 928S, mail your business card to Porsche Manager, 1940 Eglinton Avenue East, Scarborough, Ontario M1L 2M2.

On driving a Porsche. And other rites of passage. There is a certain inevitability to some drivers about owning a Porsche. For them, it is never a matter of whether to own one or not. It is simply a matter of when.

This has to do, of course, with the kinds of people who own Porsches, and their attitudes towards automobiles.

Certainly, they have never viewed cars simply as transportation. They love them and the driving of them for their own sake. Automobiles that you drive, not merely navigate.

And when they experience for the first time the handling and performance of the Porsche 944, it is a pivotal experience, akin to other significant events that occur in one's life, events that have the quality of bringing about change and fulfillment.

Why is this so? The individuals who drive Porsches would be bewildered by the question.

It simply is.

Such people are drawn to Porsche as surely as a compass needle is drawn to magnetic north. And just as surely, they will find it.

Priced under $35,000. For information on the 944, send your business card to Porsche Division, 1940 Eglinton Avenue East, Scarborough, Ontario M1L 2M2.

MERIT
ART DIRECTION

CONSUMER MAGAZINE AD

AWARDED TO
  Allan Kazmer / Paul Cade
CREATIVE DIRECTOR / WRITER
  Allan Kazmer
ART DIRECTOR
  Paul Cade
PHOTOGRAPHER
  Nigel Dickson
ADVERTISING AGENCY
  Doyle Dane Bernbach Advertising Ltd.
CLIENT
  Midland Doherty Ltd.

CONSUMER MAGAZINE AD

AWARDED TO
  Allan Kazmer / Steve Thursby
CREATIVE DIRECTOR / WRITER
  Allan Kazmer
ART DIRECTOR
  Steve Thursby
PHOTOGRAPHER
  Nigel Dickson
ADVERTISING AGENCY
  Doyle Dane Bernbach Advertising Ltd.
CLIENT
  Midland Doherty Ltd.

MERIT

ART DIRECTION

CONSUMER MAGAZINE AD

AWARDED TO ART DIRECTOR / DESIGNER
  Jerry Wiese
CREATIVE DIRECTOR / WRITER
  Faye Fonzlow
PHOTOGRAPHER
  Ivor Sharp
PRODUCTION SUPERVISOR
  Gary Stone
ADVERTISING AGENCY
  J. Walter Thompson Company Ltd.
CLIENT
  Ralston Purina Inc.

CONSUMER MAGAZINE AD

AWARDED TO
  Leon Berger / Paul Lavoie / Ron Caplan
  J. Walter Thompson - Montreal
CREATIVE DIRECTOR
  Leon Berger
ART DIRECTOR
  Paul Lavoie
PHOTOGRAPHER
  Larry Williams
WRITER
  Ron Caplan
ADVERTISING AGENCY
  J. Walter Thompson - Montreal
CLIENT
  Kraft Limited

ART DIRECTION 23

MERIT
ART DIRECTION

CONSUMER MAGAZINE AD - SERIES
AWARDED TO
  Hayhurst Communications Alberta Limited
CREATIVE DIRECTOR
  Trevor McConnell
ILLUSTRATOR
  Michael Dangelmeyer
ADVERTISING AGENCY
  Hayhurst Communications Alberta Limited
CLIENT
  Trans Alta Utilities Corporation

MERIT

ART DIRECTION

CONSUMER MAGAZINE AD
AWARDED TO
  Allan Kazmer / Steve Thursby
CREATIVE DIRECTOR / WRITER
  Allan Kazmer
ART DIRECTOR / WRITER
  Steve Thursby
PHOTOGRAPHER
  Ian Campbell
TYPOGRAPHER
  Typsettra Ltd.
ADVERTISING AGENCY
  Doyle Dane Bernbach Advertising Ltd.
CLIENT
  Heineken Marketing Canada

NEWSPAPER ADVERTISEMENT
AWARDED TO
  Scali, McCabe, Sloves (Canada) Ltd.
CREATIVE DIRECTOR / ART DIRECTOR
  Gary E. Prouk / Andre Morkel
PHOTOGRAPHER / RETOUCHER
  Stanley Wong / Lou Normandeau
TYPOGRAPHER
  Typsettra Ltd.
WRITER
  Brian Quennell
ADVERTISING AGENCY
  Scali, McCabe, Sloves (Canada) Ltd.
CLIENT
  Apple Canada Inc.

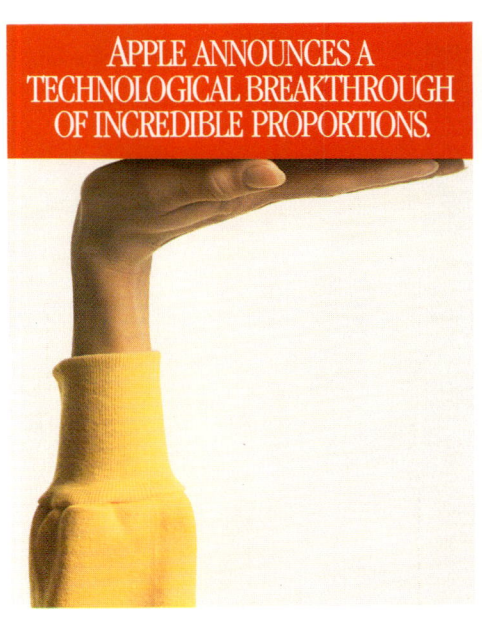

ART DIRECTION

MERIT
ART DIRECTION

QUEST SEPARATES THE URBANE FROM THE URBAN.

It is not by accident that people who make our cities worth reading about read Quest. In fact, Quest readers' intense involvements in and loyalties to the magazine are based on a lovely bit of circular logic.

Publish a magazine that deals with the real and changing issues that affect the quality of life in our cities. And then, deliver it by mail to the very people who contribute to that quality. Thus Quest's contents reflect the readers. The readers intuitively reflect on the contents. And the circle is unbroken.

In the past 10 years, the Quest circle has not only remained unbroken, it has changed dramatically in size and scope. "Change" being the operative word. As the cities changed, Quest changed. Following the population rush to 21 major cities, Quest flourishes in these 21 cities, reaching a far greater audience than those who consider us their competition. Anticipating the rising educational achievements of its city dwellers, Quest journalists challenged their urbane readers with the larger issues of the day. Telling the "what". But probing the "why".

Appealing equally to the sexes, the Quest mailbag is filled monthly with prosaic letters of praise or articulate condemnation from both genders. With urbanity the only common thread.

As for an economic skew, Quest readers tend to be the Joneses, rather than the people trying to keep up with them.

As for similar publications, quite candidly, there are none. If this seems immodest, we invite the reader to name one. True, two fine weekly newsmagazines do have a general appeal to our urban population. Yet only Quest separates the urbane from the urban.

QUEST
Urban renewal for the city mind.

CONSUMER MAGAZINE AD - SERIES

AWARDED TO
Allan Kazmer / Paul Cade
CREATIVE DIRECTOR
Allan Kazmer
ART DIRECTOR / ILLUSTRATOR
Paul Cade
WRITER
Allan Kazmer
PRODUCTION SUPERVISOR
Tom Poole
ADVERTISING AGENCY
Doyle Dane Bernbach Advertising Ltd.
CLIENT
Comac Communications – Quest Magazine

THE PEOPLE WHO MAKE OUR CITY WORTH READING ABOUT, READ QUEST.

Quest readers are a fascinating lot. All one million five hundred thousand of them. And lest you think we exaggerate or pander to their egos, consider the following.

An important and vital city is simply a composite of the important and vital people who reside therein. Be they architects, teachers, poets, politicians (yes, politicians) lawmakers or lawyers, captains of industry or captains of hockey teams.

These are the very people Quest magazine is written to, for and quite often about. So far, so good.

Then, using a clever bit of demographic sleuthing, Quest is delivered by mail to most of these selfsame people. It is a marriage of contents and readers made in heaven. Rarely does a journalist (or an advertiser for that matter) have an opportunity to speak in such a selective way to such a large and selected audience. No wonder then that Quest magazine has so many more primary readers than the general news magazines. When the readers you choose to circulate to are your primary concern, you end up with an awful lot of primary readers.

In fact, as curious as it may seem and for reasons known only to themselves, almost a third of all urban adults in 35-thousand-dollar plus households do not subscribe to a single magazine. Not a one. This urbane and affluent group, we might point out, has no aversion whatsoever to reading their free copy of Quest. Actually, many of them have graciously pointed out that "Quest is one of the few things in life affluent people ever get for free". This reaching the unreachable gives Quest additional primary readers no subscription magazine has yet found a way to penetrate.

So, in quiet conclusion, it must be said that if you are seriously looking for the people who make our cities worth reading about, you'll find them reading Quest.

QUEST
Urban renewal for the city mind.

CONSUMER MAGAZINE AD - SERIES

AWARDED TO
Allan Kazmer / Paul Cade
CREATIVE DIRECTOR
Allan Kazmer
ART DIRECTOR / ILLUSTRATOR
Paul Cade
WRITER
Allan Kazmer
PRODUCTION SUPERVISOR
Tom Poole
ADVERTISING AGENCY
Doyle Dane Bernbach Advertising Ltd.
CLIENT
Comac Communications – Quest Magazine

MERIT

ART DIRECTION

CONSUMER MAGAZINE AD - SERIES

AWARDED TO
Allan Kazmer / Paul Cade
CREATIVE DIRECTOR
Allan Kazmer
ART DIRECTOR
Paul Cade
ILLUSTRATOR
Miro Malish
WRITER
Allan Kazmer
PRODUCTION SUPERVISOR
Tom Poole
ADVERTISING AGENCY
Doyle Dane Bernbach Advertising Ltd.
CLIENT
Comac Communications – Quest Magazine
YEAR OF PRODUCTION 1984

Quest arms the pragmatic, stimulates the romantic, amazes the logical, encourages the intuitive and challenges the journalist.

Other than that, it's just a slick, glossy urban rag.

QUEST
Urban renewal for the city mind.

CONSUMER MAGAZINE AD - SERIES

AWARDED TO
Allan Kazmer / Paul Cade
CREATIVE DIRECTOR
Allan Kazmer
ART DIRECTOR
Paul Cade
ILLUSTRATOR
John Martin
WRITER
Allan Kazmer
PRODUCTION SUPERVISOR
Tom Poole
ADVERTISING AGENCY
Doyle Dane Bernbach Advertising Ltd.
CLIENT
Comac Communications – Quest Magazine
YEAR OF PRODUCTION 1984

QUEST. URBAN RENEWAL FOR THE CITY MIND.

Of all the minds in the whole world, the city mind needs the most attention. The most care and feeding. The most stimuli. The most rest and relaxation. Failure to regularly renew the city mind can, if you're not careful, result in a myriad of negative syndromes, ranging from mental urban blight to split-level thinking. (Egads!)

Fortunately, antidotes do exist. And one of the most commonly used antidotes by the bulk of urbane, urban dwellers is a good session with Quest Magazine. Written to, for and sometimes about the very people who make our cities worth reading about, Quest is then delivered, by mail, to most of those selfsame people. And their numbers are vast. So vast, in fact, that Quest delivers a larger audience in all of this country's 21 major urban centres than any of our competition.

Definitely not a newsmagazine (news often being the very reason why the need for mental urban renewal), Quest deals primarily with issues. Social issues. Political issues. Aesthetic issues. Moral issues. Human issues. And it deals with these issues in a thoughtful, probing and ofttimes whimsical manner. Not surprisingly, the level of Quest journalism accurately reflects the level of education of Quest readers, uncommonly high and usually enriched by a good dose of "street smarts". Income levels, travel and participation in the arts are also uncommonly high, making Quest readers eager recipients of essays on these and related areas.

Now, if by chance, you have a message about a product or service that logically relates to this vast yet special group and have heretofore not published that message within the pages of Quest, may we gently make this suggestion. Perhaps, just perhaps, your media plan might profit from a little urban renewal of its own.

QUEST

MERIT
ART DIRECTION

CONSUMER MAGAZINE AD - SERIES
AWARDED TO
  Allan Kazmer / Paul Cade
CREATIVE DIRECTOR
  Allan Kazmer
ART DIRECTOR
  Paul Cade
PHOTOGRAPHER
  Nigel Dickson
WRITER
  Allan Kazmer
ADVERTISING AGENCY
  Doyle Dane Bernbach Advertising Ltd.
CLIENT
  Midland Doherty Ltd.

MERIT

ART DIRECTION

CONSUMER MAGAZINE AD - SERIES
AWARDED TO
Allan Kazmer / Paul Cade
CREATIVE DIRECTOR
Allan Kazmer
ART DIRECTOR
Paul Cade
PHOTOGRAPHER
Nigel Dickson
WRITER
Allan Kazmer
ADVERTISING AGENCY
Doyle Dane Bernbach Advertising Ltd.
CLIENT
Midland Doherty Ltd.

ART DIRECTION 29

MERIT
ART DIRECTION

NEWSPAPER ADVERTISEMENT
AWARDED TO
  Terry Iles
CREATIVE DIRECTOR
  Gary E. Prouk
ART DIRECTOR
  Terry Iles
ILLUSTRATOR
  Doug Panton
TYPOGRAPHER
  Typsettra Ltd.
WRITER
  Steve Catlin
ADVERTISING AGENCY
  Scali, McCabe, Sloves (Canada) Ltd.
CLIENT
  Ralston Purina Canada Inc.

NEWSPAPER ADVERTISEMENT
AWARDED TO
  Scali, McCabe, Sloves (Canada) Ltd.
CREATIVE DIRECTOR
  Gary E. Prouk
ART DIRECTOR
  Andre Morkel
PHOTOGRAPHER
  Bruce Horn / Mark Coppos
RETOUCHER
  Lou Normandeau
TYPOGRAPHER
  Typsettra Ltd.
WRITER
  Brian Quennell
ADVERTISING AGENCY
  Scali, McCabe, Sloves (Canada) Ltd.
CLIENT
  Apple Canada Inc.

30 GRAPHIC EXCELLENCE

MERIT

ART DIRECTION

TRADE PUBLICATION AD - SERIES
AWARDED TO
  Jane Pritchard
CREATIVE DIRECTOR / ART DIRECTOR
  Jane Pritchard
DESIGNER
  Jane Pritchard
ILLUSTRATOR / ARTIST
  Kent Smith
TYPOGRAPHER
  Typsettra Ltd.
WRITER
  Bill Martin
ADVERTISING AGENCY
  J. Walter Thompson Company Ltd.
CLIENT
  Labatt's Ontario Breweries

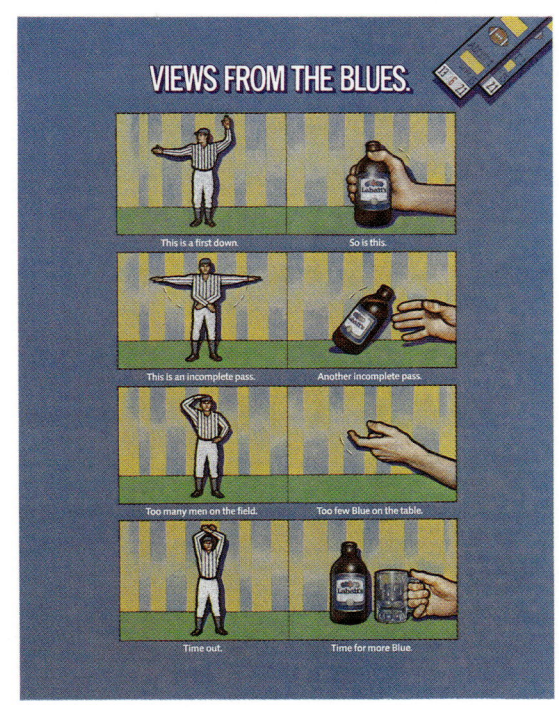

ART DIRECTION 31

MERIT
ART DIRECTION

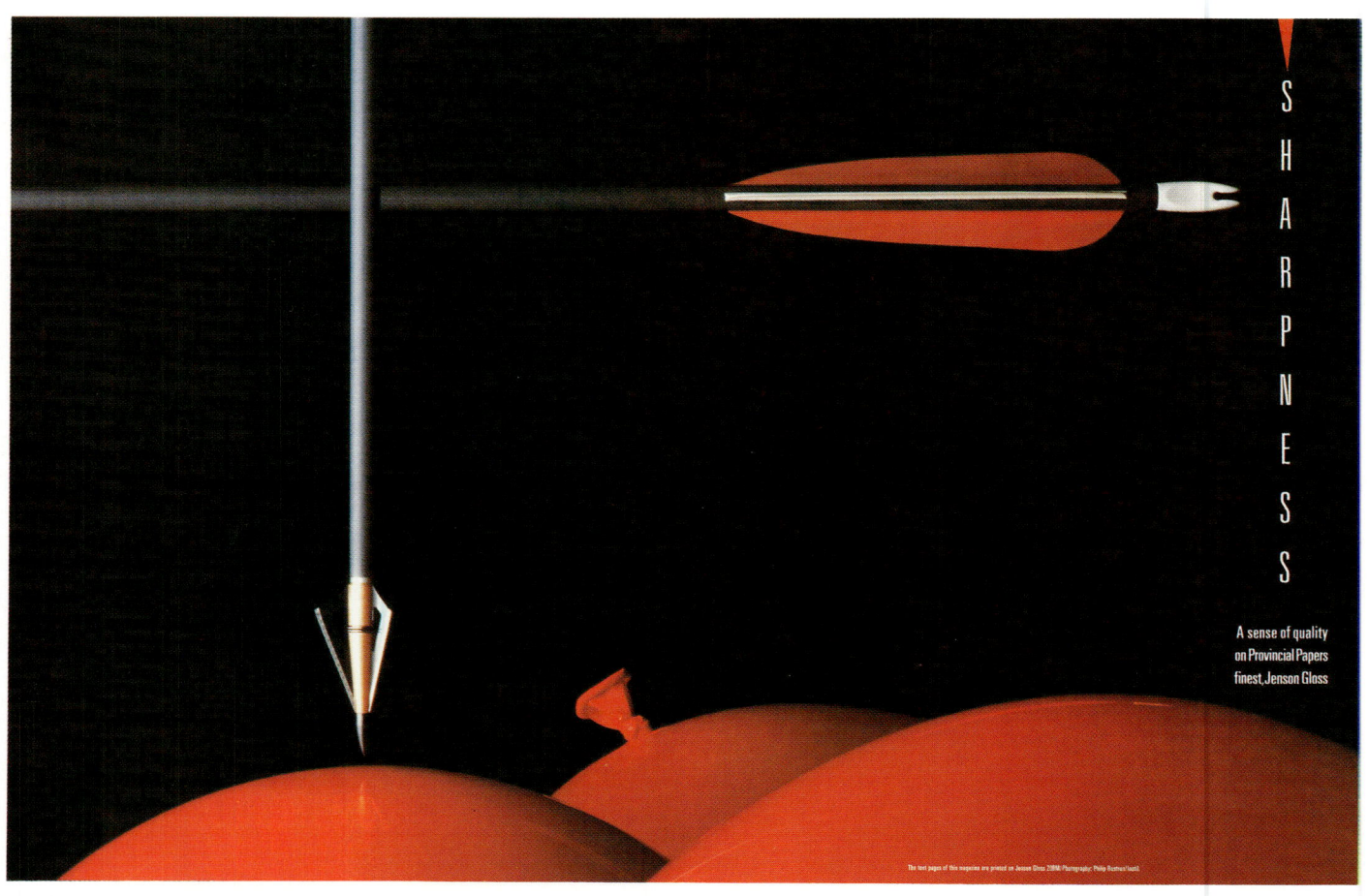

ADVERTISING PHOTOGRAPHY

AWARDED TO
  Vopni & Parsons Design Ltd.
CREATIVE DIRECTOR
  Jon Vopni
ART DIRECTORS / DESIGNERS
  Jon Vopni / Sandra Parsons
PHOTOGRAPHER
  Philip Rostron / Instil
COLOUR SEPARATOR
  Herzig Sommerville, Ltd.
CLIENT
  Provincial Papers

PUBLIC SERVICE AD

AWARDED TO CREATIVE DIRECTORS
  Jim Ramsden / Wayne Bosada
ART DIRECTOR / DESIGNER
  Jim Ramsden
ADVERTISING AGENCY
  Vickers & Benson
CLIENT
  Muscular Dystrophy Assoc. of Canada

MERIT

ART DIRECTION

ADVERTISING ILLUSTRATION

AWARDED TO
  Jane Pritchard
CREATIVE DIRECTOR / ART DIRECTOR
  Jane Pritchard
ILLUSTRATOR / ARTIST
  Roger Hill
TYPOGRAPHER
  Typsettra Ltd.
COLOUR SEPARATOR
  H & S Reliance
ADVERTISING AGENCY
  J. Walter Thompson Company Ltd.
CLIENT
  Labatt's Ontario Breweries

ADVERTISING PHOTOGRAPHY

AWARDED TO
  Vopni & Parsons Design Limited
ART DIRECTORS / DESIGNERS
  Jon Vopni / Sandra Parsons
PHOTOGRAPHER
  Philip Rostron / Instil
PRINTER
  Baker Gurney & McLaren Press
  Silkscreen, Holland & Neil
CLIENT
  Provincial Papers

MERIT

ART DIRECTION

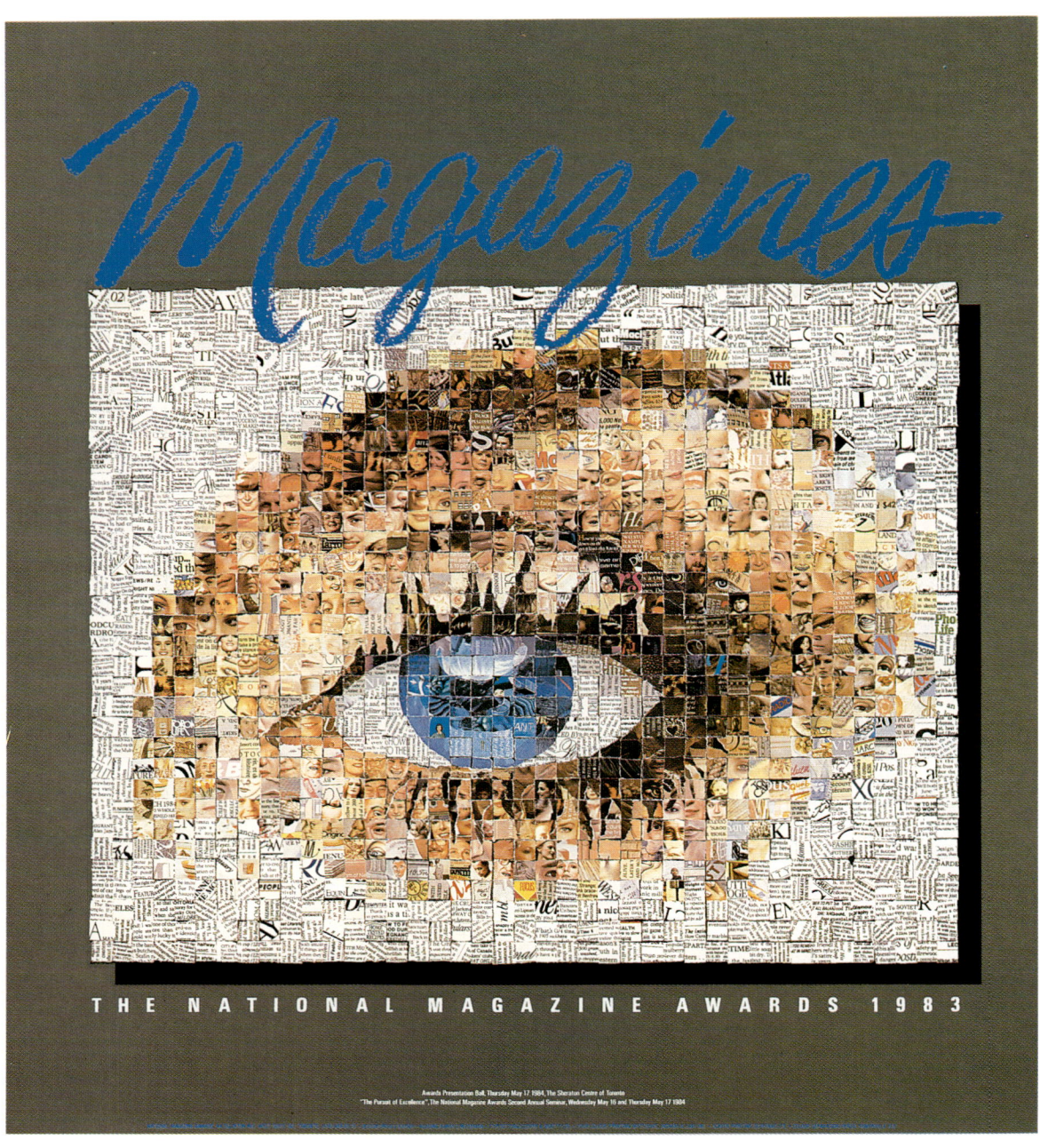

ADVERTISING ILLUSTRATION
AWARDED TO
  Ursula Kaiser
CREATIVE DIRECTOR / ART DIRECTOR
  Ursula Kaiser
DESIGNER / ILLUSTRATOR
  Ursula Kaiser
HEADING
  Karen Cheeseman
PRINTER
  Matthews Ingham & Lake Inc.,
  Screenad Ltd.
COLOUR SEPARATOR
  Herzig Somerville, Ltd.
CLIENT
  National Magazine Awards Foundation

MERIT

ART DIRECTION

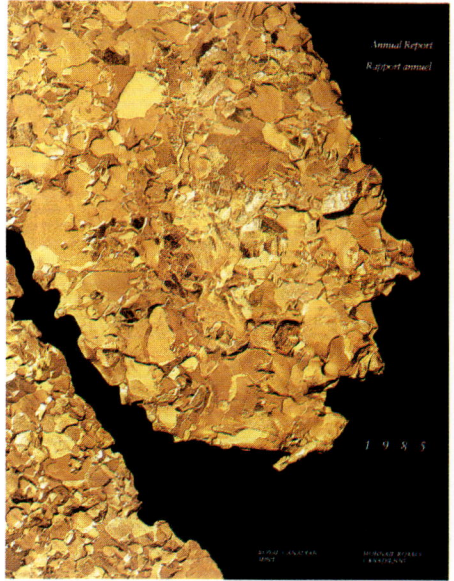

ANNUAL REPORT

AWARDED TO
 Furman Graphic Design
CREATIVE / ART DIRECTOR / DESIGNER
 Aviva Furman
PHOTOGRAPHER
 Davidson Bénard Group
TYPOGRAPHER
 M & H Typography Ltd.
PRODUCTION STUDIO
 Furman Graphic Design
PRINTER
 Arthurs-Jones Lithographing
COLOUR SEPARATOR
 Empress Graphics Inc.
CLIENT
 Royal Canadian Mint

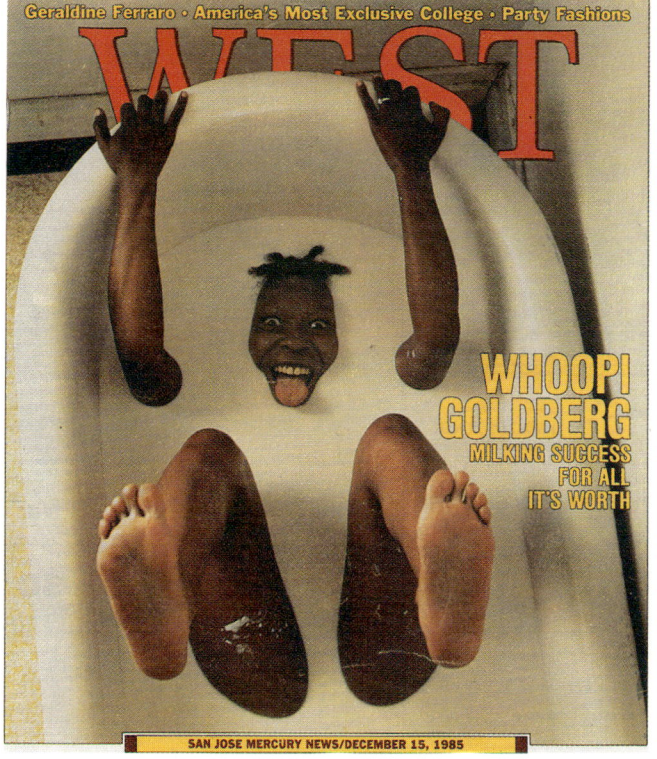

MAGAZINE COVER

AWARDED TO
 Bambi Nicklen
CREATIVE DIRECTOR / ART DIRECTOR
 Bambi Nicklen
PHOTOGRAPHER
 Annie Leibovitz
TYPOGRAPHER
 Bambi Nicklen
EDITOR
 Jeffrey Klein
PUBLISHER
 WEST Magazine, San Jose Mercury News

ART DIRECTION 35

MERIT
ART DIRECTION

BROCHURE
AWARDED TO
  Terry O Communications Inc.
CREATIVE DIRECTOR / ART DIRECTOR
  Terry O'Connor
DESIGNERS
  Terry O'Connor/Helena Fong O'Connor
PHOTOGRAPHER
  Jay Jackson
PRINTER
  Herzig Sommerville, Ltd.
CLIENT
  Sheridan College

OUTDOOR TRANSIT AD
AWARDED TO
  Jane Pritchard
CREATIVE DIRECTOR / ART DIRECTOR
  Jane Pritchard
DESIGNER
  Jane Pritchard
WRITER
  Bill Lower
ADVERTISING AGENCY
  J. Walter Thompson Company Ltd.
CLIENT
  Labatt's Ontario Breweries

36 GRAPHIC EXCELLENCE

MERIT

ART DIRECTION

MAGAZINE COVER
AWARDED TO
 Nick Burnett
ART DIRECTOR
 Nick Burnett
ILLUSTRATOR
 Rick Fischer

CATALOGUE
AWARDED TO
 Charles Michael Helmken
CREATIVE DIRECTOR / EDITOR
 Charles Michael Helmken
ART DIRECTOR / DESIGNER
 Ikko Tanaka
PHOTOGRAPHER
 Ikko Tanaka Design Studio
PRINTER
 Dai-Nippon Printing Co. Ltd., Tokyo
CLIENT / PUBLISHER
 The Shoshin Society

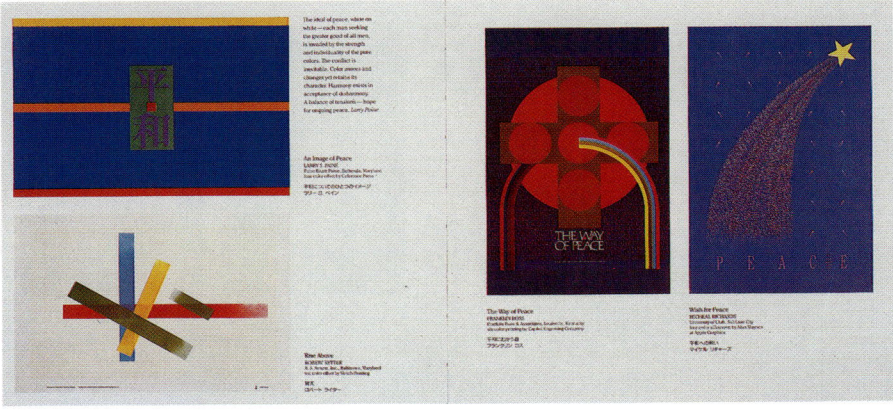

ART DIRECTION 37

MERIT

ART DIRECTION

OUTDOOR TRANSIT AD - SERIES
AWARDED TO
  Scali, McCabe, Sloves (Canada) Ltd.
CREATIVE DIRECTORS
  Gary E. Prouk / Yves Simard
ART DIRECTOR
  Johanne Allard
ILLUSTRATORS
  Helmut Langeder / Alain Massicotte
  Catalpa Design
WRITER
  Luc Merineau
ADVERTISING AGENCY
  Scali, McCabe, Sloves (Canada) Ltd.
CLIENT
  Cadbury Schweppes Canada

MERIT

ART DIRECTION

OUTDOOR TRANSIT AD
AWARDED TO
 Allan Kazmer / Steve Thursby
CREATIVE DIRECTOR
 Allan Kazmer
ART DIRECTOR
 Steve Thursby
ILLUSTRATOR
 Desmond Montague
TYPOGRAPHER
 Typsettra Ltd.
WRITER
 Allan Kazmer
PRODUCTION SUPERVISOR
 John Stevenson
ADVERTISING AGENCY
 Doyle Dane Bernbach Advertising Ltd.
CLIENT
 Levi Strauss

OUTDOOR TRANSIT AD
AWARDED TO
 Jim Burt
CREATIVE DIRECTOR
 Graham Watt
ART DIRECTOR / DESIGNER
 Jim Burt
ILLUSTRATOR
 Bob Browning
WRITER
 Graham Watt
COLOUR SEPARATOR
 Herzig Somerville, Ltd.
ADVERTISING AGENCY
 McKim/Watt Burt
CLIENT
 Ontario Milk Marketing Board

MERIT
ART DIRECTION

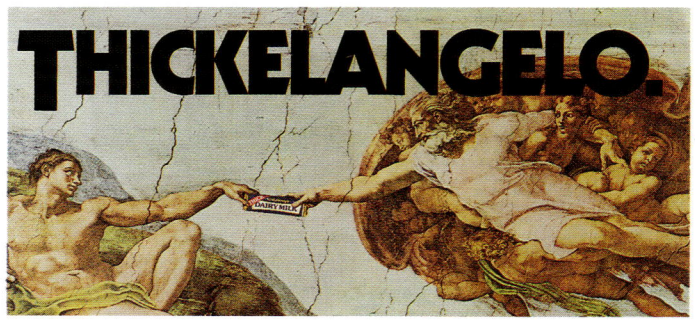
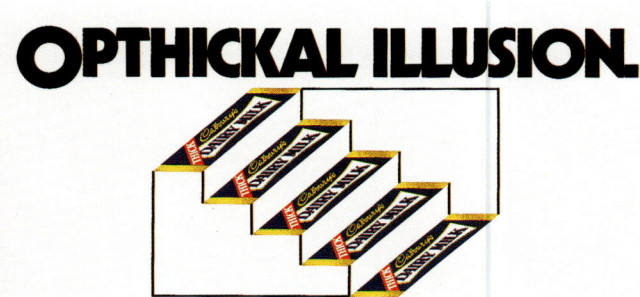

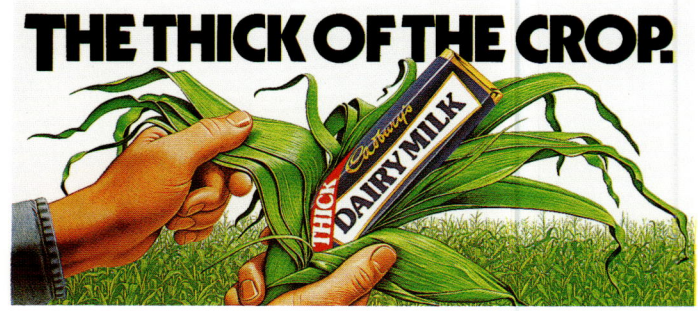

OUTDOOR TRANSIT AD - SERIES

AWARDED TO
  Scali, McCabe, Sloves (Canada) Ltd.
CREATIVE DIRECTOR
  Gary E. Prouk
ART DIRECTORS
  Gray Abraham / Michael Fromowitz
ILLUSTRATORS
  Julius Ciss / Fausto Mourato
  Martin Hyde / G. Gauntlett
  Michelangelo Buonarroti / Christine Bunn
WRITERS
  Gary E. Prouk / Hans Olaf Ein

PHOTOGRAPHER
  Nigel Dickson
RETOUCHER
  Bob Carmen
ADVERTISING AGENCY
  Scali, McCabe, Sloves (Canada) Ltd.
CLIENT
  Cadbury Scheweppes Canada

MERIT

ART DIRECTION

We have more loafers than the Argos' defence. *There are 302 stores in The Great Indoors.*	We have enough sweaters to cut Toronto's heating bill 3%. *There are 302 stores in The Great Indoors.*
We sell more records than Anne Murray. *There are 302 stores in The Great Indoors.*	We have a pair of oxfords for every scholar at U. of T. *There are 302 stores in The Great Indoors.*
We have enough pin-stripes to suit every banker on Bay Street. *There are 302 stores in The Great Indoors.*	We have enough bathing suits for everyone in the Beaches. *There are 302 stores in The Great Indoors.*
We could feed a sell-out crowd at the Gardens. *There are 302 stores in The Great Indoors.*	We have enough leather to supply everyone on Queen Street West. *There are 302 stores in The Great Indoors.*

OUTDOOR TRANSIT AD - SERIES
AWARDED TO
  Scali, McCabe, Sloves (Canada) Ltd.
CREATIVE DIRECTOR / ART DIRECTOR
  Gary E. Prouk / Karen Howe
WRITER
  Peter Byrne
ADVERTISING AGENCY
  Scali, McCabe, Sloves (Canada) Ltd.
CLIENT
  The Eaton Centre

CHAPTER 2
GRAPHIC EXCELLENCE

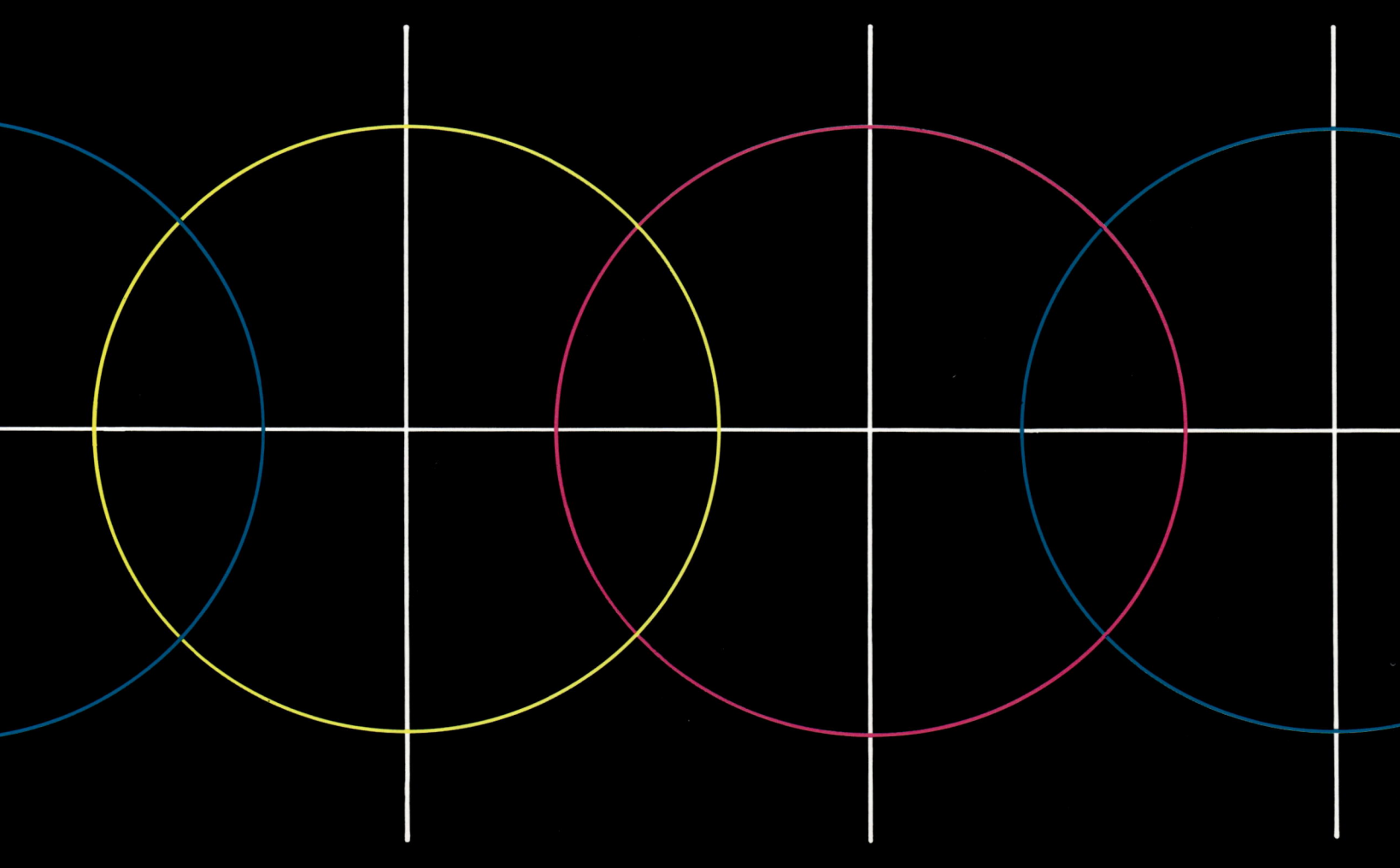

GRAPHIC DESIGN

Designations in this category include logo design, advertising poster, brochure—series, complete book, annual report, stationery, brochure, catalogue, magazine cover, postage stamp, greeting card, promotional, and self-promotional.

Diverse subject matter, media, type style, and composition make for striking logos and brochures, while bright, colorful photographs contribute to impressive annual reports. The many outstanding selections convey the eloquence with which good graphic design can communicate a message.

GOLD

GRAPHIC DESIGN

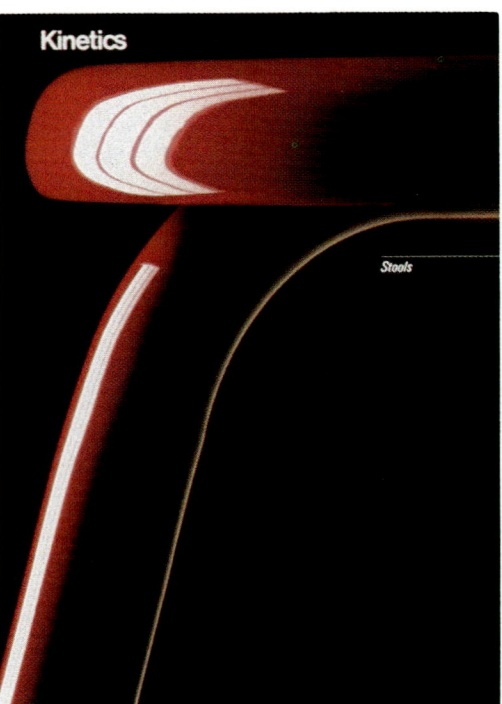

GOLD

GRAPHIC DESIGN

BROCHURE - SERIES

AWARDED TO
 Taylor & Browning Design Associates
ART DIRECTOR
 Paul Browning
DESIGNER
 Scott Taylor / Paul Browning
 Sharon Lockwood / Terry Montag
 Joe Drvaric / Philip Brazeau
PHOTOGRAPHER
 Pat LaCroix
TYPOGRAPHER
 Type Studio
WRITER
 David Parry
PRINTER
 Matthews, Ingham & Lake Inc.
CLIENT
 Kinetics Furniture

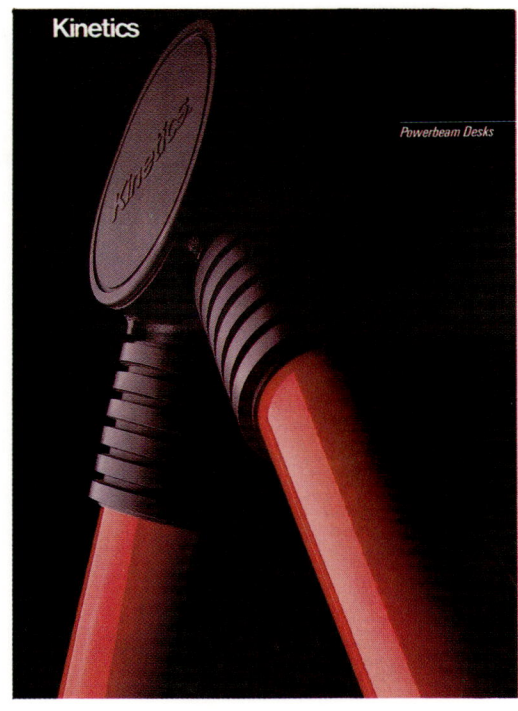

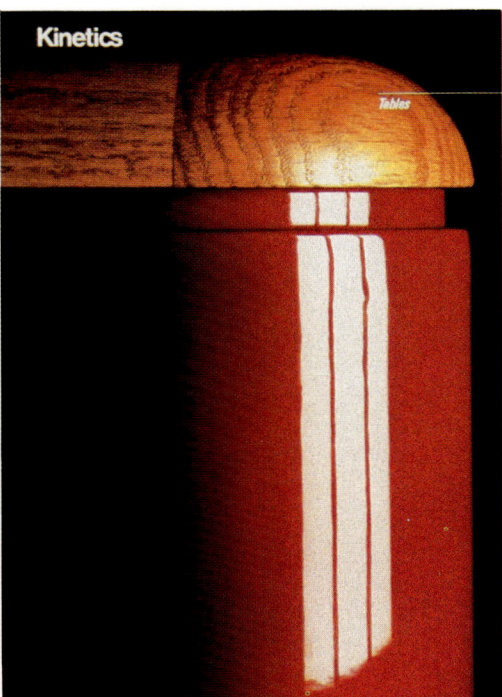

SILVER

GRAPHIC DESIGN

LOGO DESIGN

AWARDED TO
 Neville Smith
CREATIVE DIRECTOR / ART DIRECTOR
 Neville Smith
DESIGNER / ILLUSTRATOR
 Neville Smith
PRODUCTION STUDIO
 Neville Smith Graphic Design
CLIENT
 Black Cat Cafe

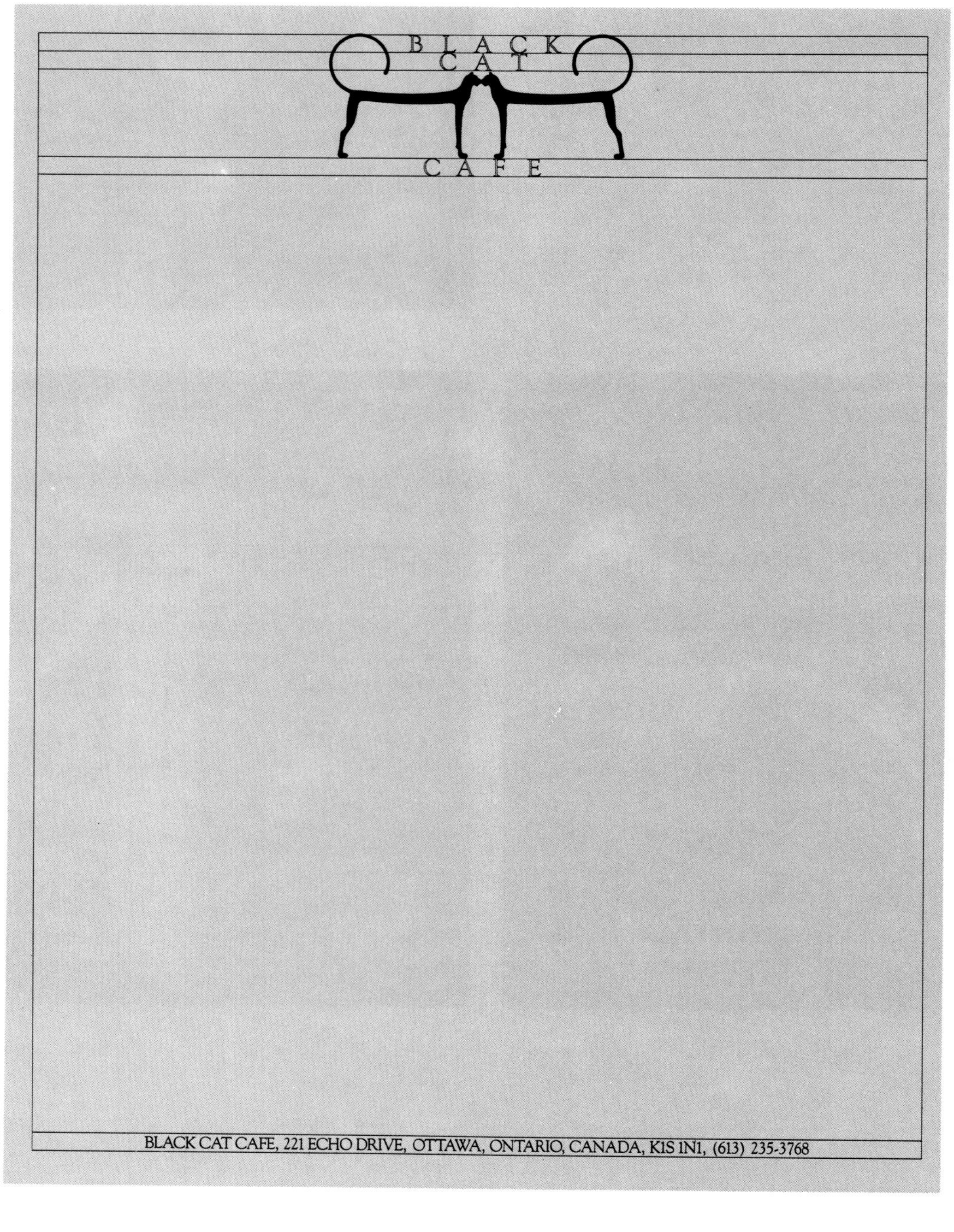

SILVER

GRAPHIC DESIGN

ADVERTISING POSTER

AWARDED TO
Neville Smith
CREATIVE DIRECTOR / ART DIRECTOR
Neville Smith
DESIGNER / ILLUSTRATOR
Neville Smith
TYPOGRAPHER
A.P.H. Typesetting
PRODUCTION STUDIO
Neville Smith Graphic Design
PRINTER
Viki Ball Screen Printing
CLIENT
Black Cat Cafe

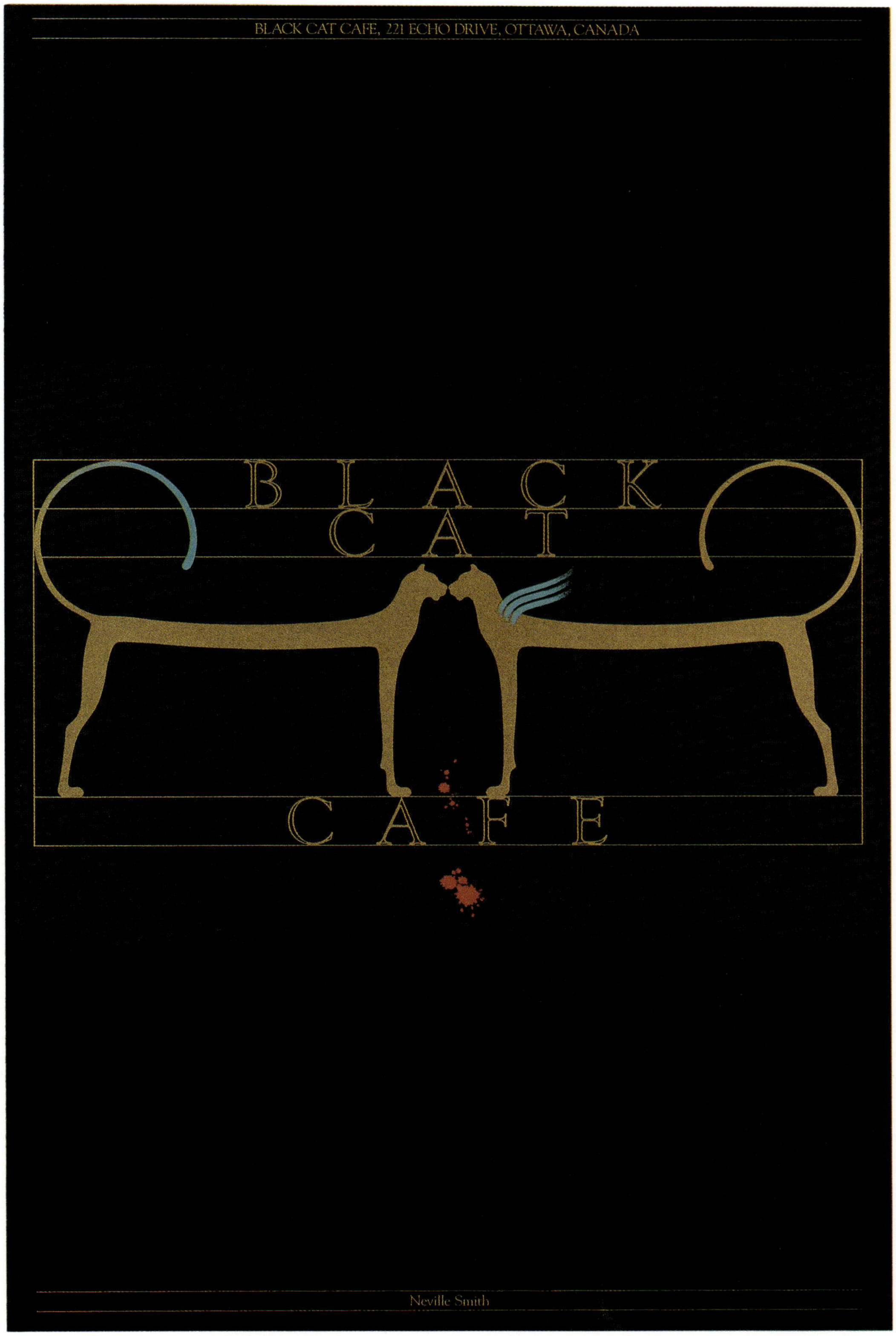

SILVER

GRAPHIC DESIGN

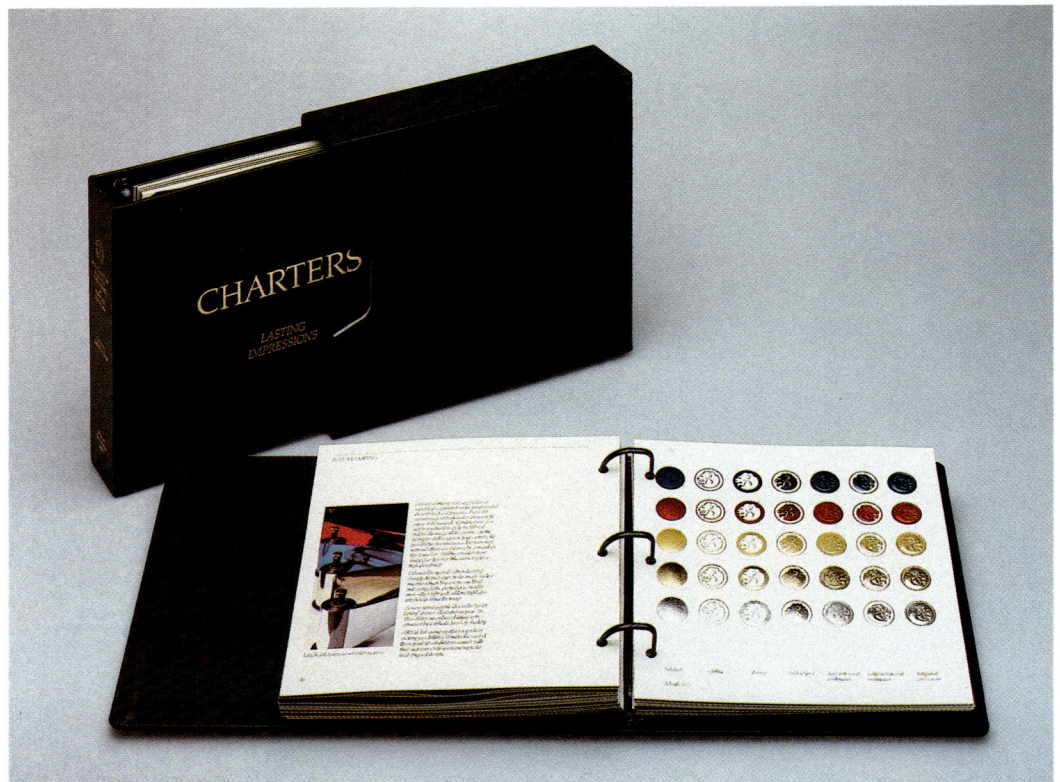

COMPLETE BOOK

AWARDED TO
  Robert Hyland Design & Associates
ART DIRECTOR
  Robert Hyland
DESIGNERS
  Jon Vopni / Robert Hyland
PHOTOGRAPHER
  Peter Christopher
ILLUSTRATORS
  Jon Vopni / George Kay
  Larry Bloss / Frank Bonigut
  Alf Ebsen
TYPOGRAPHER
  Type Studio Limited
WRITER
  David Parry / James Hynes
PRINTER
  M.C. Charters & Co. Ltd.
  Herzig Somerville Limited
COLOUR SEPARATOR
  Herzig Somerville Limited
DESIGN FIRM
  Robert Hyland Design & Associates
CLIENT
  M.C. Charters & Co. Ltd.

ANNUAL REPORT

AWARDED TO
  Grafik Communications, Ltd.
CREATIVE DIRECTOR
  Judy Kirpich
ART DIRECTOR / DESIGNER
  Susan English
ILLUSTRATOR
  Gary Kelley
ADVERTISING AGENCY
  Grafik Communications, Ltd.
CLIENT
  VM Software, Inc.

48 GRAPHIC EXCELLENCE

SILVER

GRAPHIC DESIGN

BROCHURES - SERIES
AWARDED TO
  Arnold Goodwin, Goodwin, Knab & Co.
ART DIRECTOR / DESIGNER
  Arnold Goodwin
PHOTOGRAPHER
  Jean Moss
WRITER
  Jerry Fields
WARDROBE COORDINATOR
  Jim Powers
PRINTER
  Bradley / Hennegen
CLIENT
  H. Gene Silverberg
  Bigsby & Kruthers, Inc.

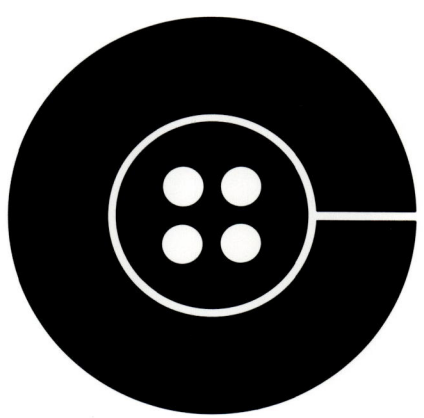

LOGO DESIGN
AWARDED TO
  Alex Gellen
CREATIVE DIRECTOR / ART DIRECTOR
  Alex Gellen
DESIGNER
  Alex Gellen
PRODUCTION STUDIO
  Alex Gellen Design
CLIENT
  Continental Fabricas

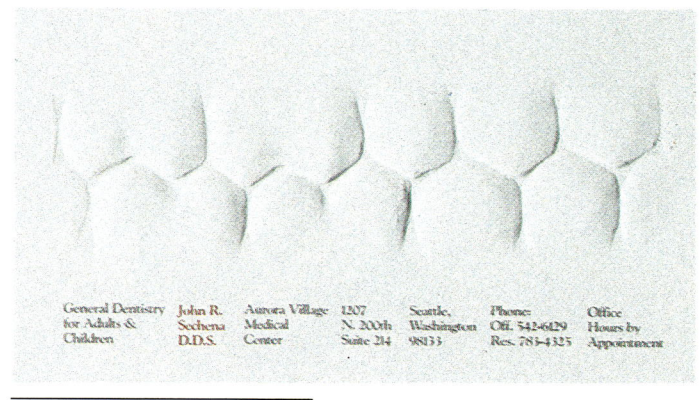

STATIONERY
AWARDED TO
  Hornall Anderson Design Works
CREATIVE DIRECTOR / ART DIRECTOR
  Jack Anderson
DESIGNER
  Jack Anderson
TYPOGRAPHER
  The Type Gallery
ADVERTISING AGENCY
  Hornall Anderson Design Works
CLIENT
  Dr. John R. Sechena

MERIT
GRAPHIC DESIGN

LOGO DESIGN

AWARDED TO
  Neville Smith
CREATIVE / ART DIRECTOR / DESIGNER
  Neville Smith
PRODUCTION STUDIO
  Neville Smith Graphic Design
CLIENT
  Starship Courier

LOGO DESIGN

AWARDED TO
  Taylor & Browning Design Associates
ART DIRECTOR / DESIGNER
  Scott Taylor
ILLUSTRATORS
  Bill Frampton / Bryan Malloy
  Karen Cheeseman
CLIENT
  Cadillac Fairview Shopping Centres

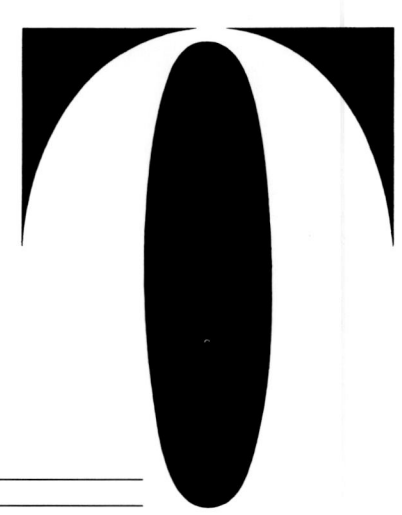

LOGO DESIGN

AWARDED TO
  Taylor & Browning Design Associates
ART DIRECTOR
  Scott Taylor
DESIGNER
  Scott Taylor / Paul Browning
CLIENT
  The Arnoldi Group Limited

LOGO DESIGN

AWARDED TO
  Terry O Communications Inc.
CREATIVE / ART DIRECTOR / DESIGNER
  Terry O'Connor
ADVERTISING AGENCY
  Terry O Communications Inc.

MERIT

GRAPHIC DESIGN

LOGO DESIGN
AWARDED TO
 Frank Mayrs
DESIGNER
 Frank Mayrs
CLIENT
 Government of Hong Kong

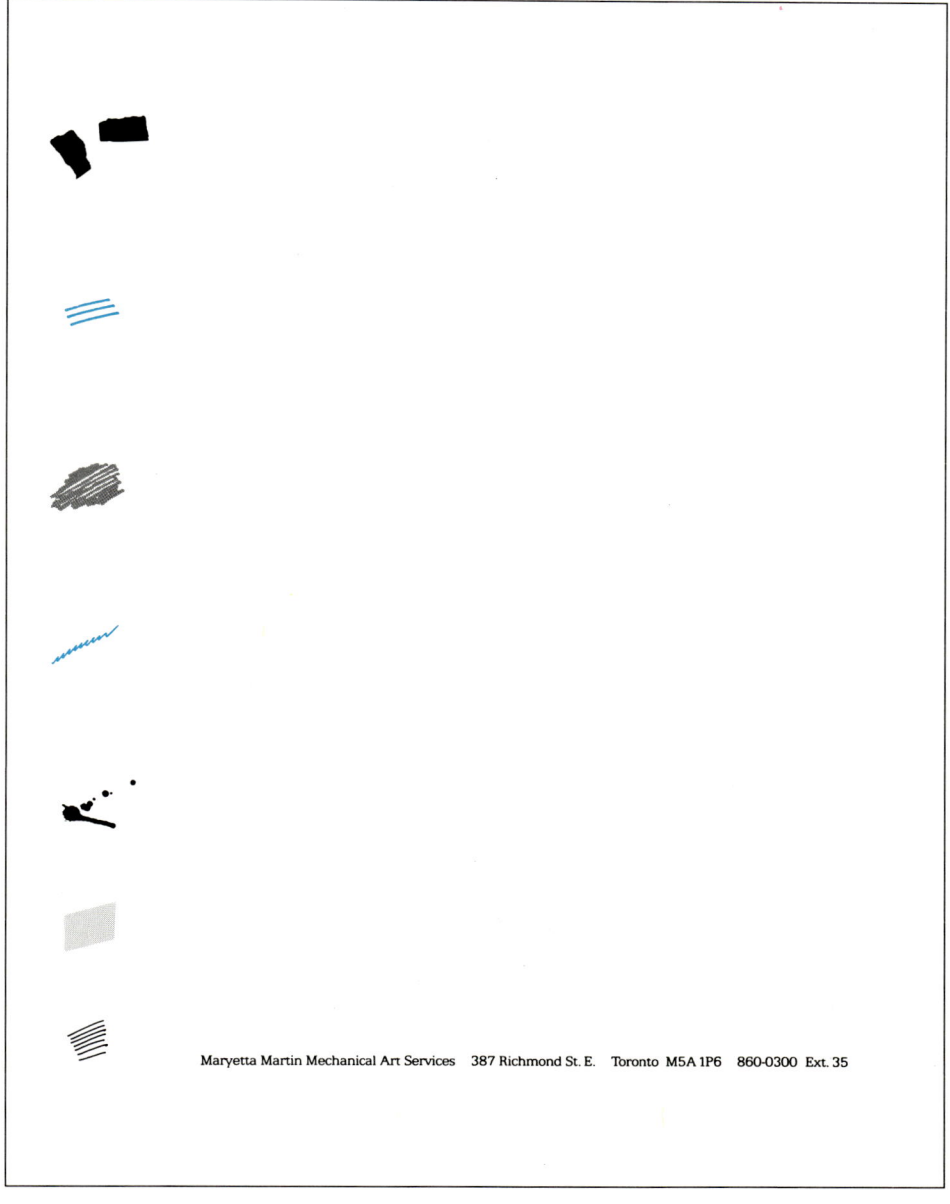

STATIONERY
AWARDED TO
 Maryetta Martin
DESIGNER
 Maryetta Martin
TYPOGRAPHER
 Cooper & Beatty, Limited
PRINTER
 Impress Printing
CLIENT
 Maryetta Martin Mechanical Art Services

MERIT
GRAPHIC DESIGN

STATIONERY

AWARDED TO
 David Johns
DESIGNER
 David Johns
ILLUSTRATOR
 S.N.G. Retouching Ltd.
TYPOGRAPHER
 Qualitype Company Ltd.
PRINTER
 Copygraph Ltd. - Letterhead/Label
 Globe Printing - Business Card
COLOUR SEPARATOR
 Bomac Batten Ltd.
CLIENT
 The Open Road Communications

MERIT

GRAPHIC DESIGN

BROCHURE

AWARDED TO
 Taylor & Browning Design Associates
ART DIRECTOR
 Scott Taylor
DESIGNER
 William Lam
PHOTOGRAPHERS
 Michel Pilon / Peter Christopher
 Rob Watson
ILLUSTRATOR
 Bill Boyko - Acorn Studio
TYPOGRAPHER
 Cooper & Beatty, Limited
PRINTER
 Matthews, Ingham & Lake Inc.
CLIENT
 Cambridge Shopping Centres

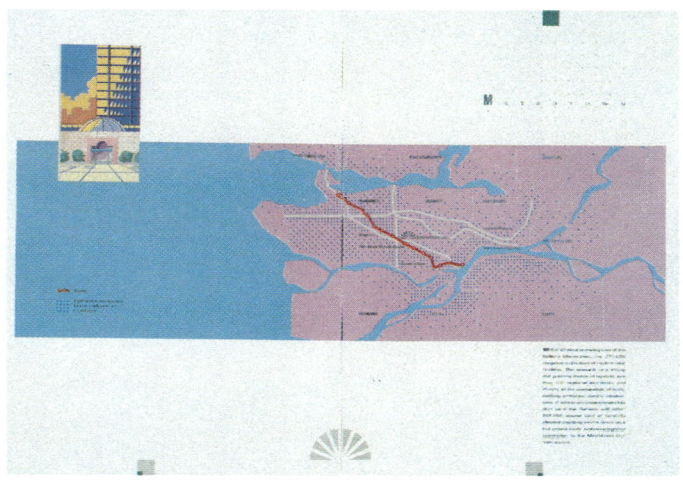

BROCHURE

AWARDED TO
 Taylor & Browning Design Associates
ART DIRECTORS
 Scott Taylor / Paul Browning
DESIGNERS
 Scott Taylor / Paul Browning
 Philip Brazeau
ILLUSTRATOR
 Steve McLachlan
TYPOGRAPHER / PRINTER
 Norgraphics (Canada) Limited
WRITER
 Jim Hynes
CLIENT
 Johnson & Higgins Willis Faber

MERIT

GRAPHIC DESIGN

BROCHURE

AWARDED TO
 Taylor & Browning Design Associates
ART DIRECTOR
 Paul Browning
DESIGNERS
 Michael Malloy / Joe Drvaric
PHOTOGRAPHER
 Pat LaCroix
TYPOGRAPHER
 Type Studio
WRITER
 David Parry
PRINTER
 Matthews, Ingham & Lake Inc.
CLIENT
 Kinetics Furniture

BROCHURE

AWARDED TO
 Taylor & Browning Design Associates
ART DIRECTOR
 Paul Browning
DESIGNERS
 Paul Browning / Scott Taylor
ILLUSTRATOR
 Steve McLachlan
TYPOGRAPHER
 Type Studio
WRITER
 David Parry
PRINTER
 Ashton Potter
CLIENT
 Kinetics Furniture

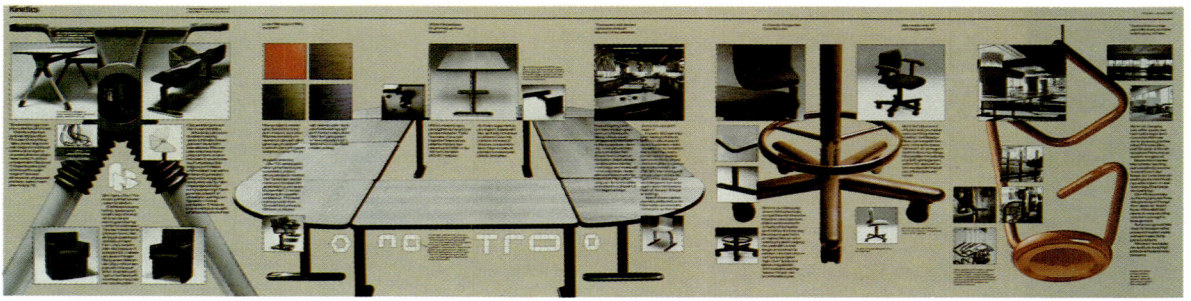

54 GRAPHIC EXCELLENCE

MERIT

GRAPHIC DESIGN

BROCHURE
AWARDED TO
  Taylor & Browning Design Associates
ART DIRECTORS
  Scott Taylor / Michael Malloy
DESIGNERS
  Michael Malloy / Derwyn Goodall
PHOTOGRAPHERS
  Peter Christopher - Location Photography
  Tim Saunders / Ian Campbell
  Product Photography
  Christopher Dew - Model Photography
ILLUSTRATOR
  Colin Brown
PRINTER
  Norgraphics (Canada) Limited
CLIENT
  Cadillac Fairview Shopping Centres

CATALOGUE
AWARDED TO
  Taylor & Browning Design Associates
ART DIRECTOR
  Paul Browning
DESIGNERS
  Catherine Haughton / Joe Drvaric
PHOTOGRAPHER
  Pat LaCroix
ILLUSTRATOR
  Joe Drvaric
TYPOGRAPHER
  Type Studio
WRITER
  David Parry
PRINTER
  Matthews, Ingham & Lake
CLIENT
  Kinetics Furniture

BROCHURE
AWARDED TO
  Taylor & Browning Design Associates
ART DIRECTORS
  Scott Taylor / Michael Malloy
DESIGNERS
  Michael Malloy / Derwyn Goodall
PHOTOGRAPHERS
  Deborah Samuel - Fashion Photography
  Christopher Dew - Model Photography
  Peter Christopher - Location Photography
ILLUSTRATORS
  Wendy Wortzman / Bill Boyko
  (Acorn Studio)
TYPOGRAPHER
  Cooper & Beatty, Limited
WRITER
  James Hynes
PRINTER
  Arthurs-Jones Lithographing Ltd.
CLIENT
  Cadillac Fairview Shopping Centres

GRAPHIC DESIGN   55

MERIT
GRAPHIC DESIGN

ANNUAL REPORT

AWARDED TO
 Taylor & Browning Design Associates
ART DIRECTOR
 Scott Taylor
DESIGNER
 John Pylypczak
PHOTOGRAPHER
 Robert Watson / Ted Horowitz
TYPOGRAPHER
 Cooper & Beatty, Limited
WRITER
 Michael Wexler
PRINTER
 Norgraphics (Canada) Limited
CLIENT
 National Business Systems Inc.

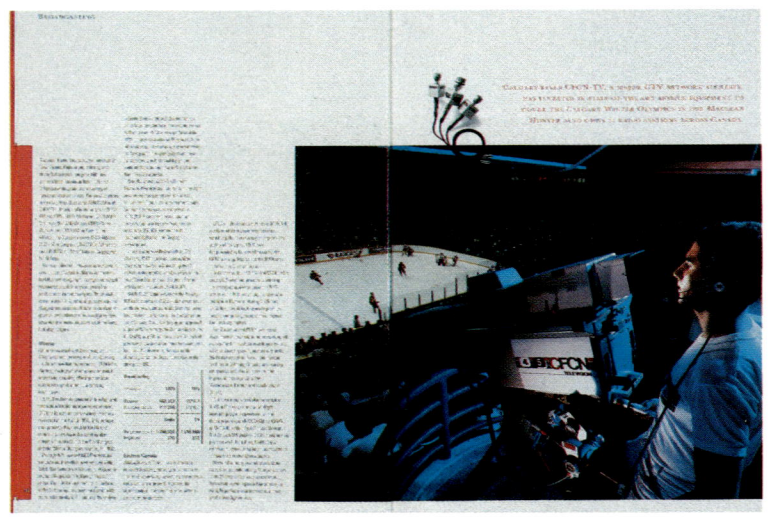

ANNUAL REPORT

AWARDED TO
 Taylor & Browning Design Associates
ART DIRECTOR
 Paul Browning
DESIGNER
 Paul Campbell
PHOTOGRAPHERS
 Paul Ornstein - Location Photography
 Ian Campbell - Studio Photography
TYPOGRAPHER
 Cooper & Beatty, Limited
WRITERS
 Jennifer Grass / James Hynes
PRINTER
 Arthurs-Jones Lithographing Ltd.
CLIENT
 Molsons Companies Limited

ANNUAL REPORT

AWARDED TO
 Taylor & Browning Design Associates
ART DIRECTOR
 Paul Browning / Scott Taylor
DESIGNER
 John Pylypczak
PHOTOGRAPHER
 Deborah MacNeil / Rob Watson
TYPOGRAPHER
 Yorkville Press Co. Ltd.
WRITER
 Colleen Flood
PRINTER
 Yorkville Press Co. Ltd.
COLOUR SEPARATOR
 Litho Plus Inc.
CLIENT
 Maclean Hunter Limited

56 GRAPHIC EXCELLENCE

MERIT

GRAPHIC DESIGN

ANNUAL REPORT

AWARDED TO
  Thomas Braise
CREATIVE DIRECTOR / PHOTOGRAPHER
  Thomas Braise
ART DIRECTOR
  Paul Schulte
DESIGNER
  Mark Anderson Design
WRITER
  Carol Westberg
PRODUCTION SUPERVISOR
  Bob Lewis
PRINTER
  Colorgraphics
CLIENT
  Fayette Manufacturing

ANNUAL REPORT

AWARDED TO
  Taylor & Browning Design Associates
ART DIRECTOR
  Paul Browning
DESIGNER
  Diti Katona
PHOTOGRAPHER
  Ian Campbell
TYPOGRAPHER
  Cooper & Beatty, Limited
WRITER
  James Hynes
PRINTER
  Arthurs-Jones Lithographing Ltd.
CLIENT
  The First Mercantile Currency Fund, Inc.

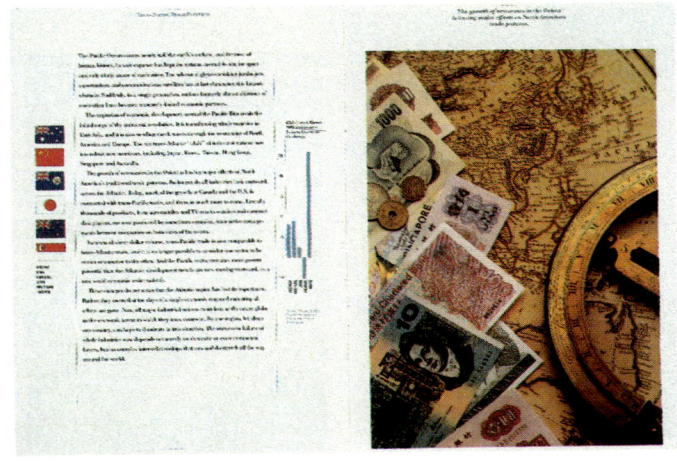

ANNUAL REPORT

AWARDED TO
  Taylor & Browning Design Associates
ART DIRECTOR
  Scott Taylor
DESIGNER
  Scott Taylor / Philip Brazeau
  Paul Browning
PHOTOGRAPHER
  Pat LaCroix
TYPOGRAPHER / PRINTER
  Norgraphics (Canada) Limited
CLIENT
  Westinghouse Canada Inc.

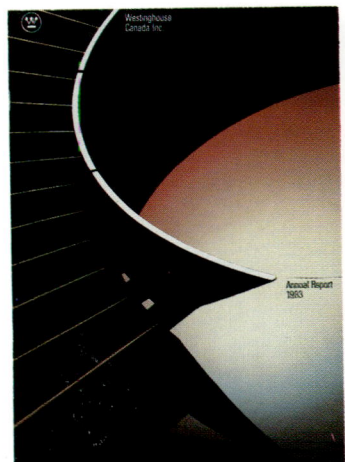
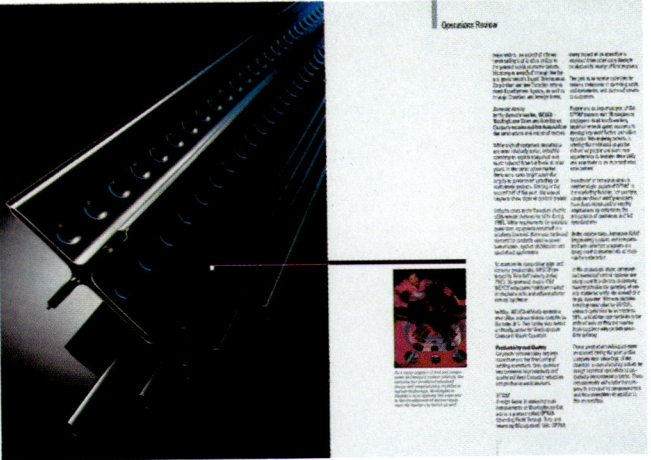

GRAPHIC DESIGN

MERIT

GRAPHIC DESIGN

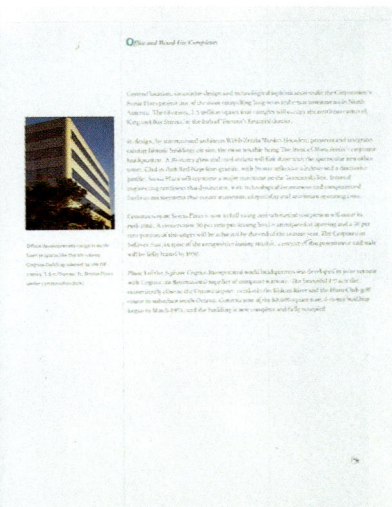

ANNUAL REPORT
AWARDED TO
 Taylor & Browning Design Associates
ART DIRECTOR
 Scott Taylor
DESIGNER
 Paul Campbell
PHOTOGRAPHER
 Peter Christopher
ILLUSTRATOR
 Derwyn Goodall
TYPOGRAPHER
 Cooper & Beatty, Limited
CLIENT
 Campeau Corporation

BOOK JACKET
AWARDED TO
 Barbara Hodgson - Douglas & McIntyre
ART DIRECTOR / DESIGNER
 Barbara Hodgson
ILLUSTRATOR
 Dave Webber
TYPOGRAPHER
 Zenith Graphics
PUBLISHER
 Douglas & McIntyre Ltd.

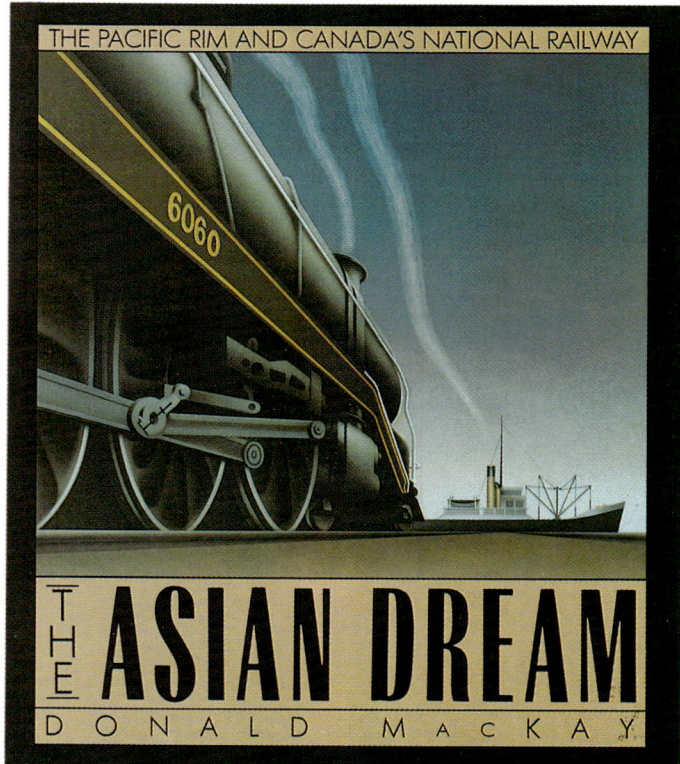

MERIT

GRAPHIC DESIGN

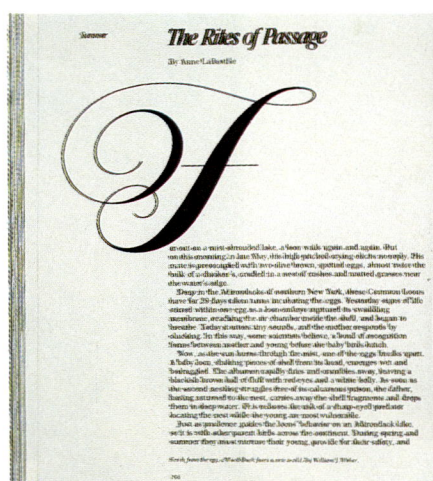

COMPLETE BOOK

AWARDED TO
 David M. Seager
ART DIRECTOR / DESIGNER
 David M. Seager
PHOTOGRAPHERS
 Stephen C. Wilson
 Karen C. Hayden (Cover)
TYPOGRAPHER
 National Geographic
PRINTER
 R.R. Donnelley & Sons, Co.
PUBLISHER
 National Geographic Society
 Beck Engraving

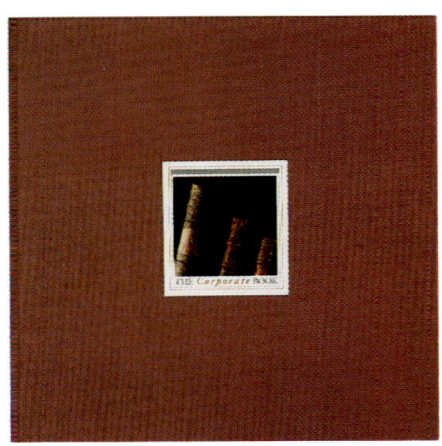
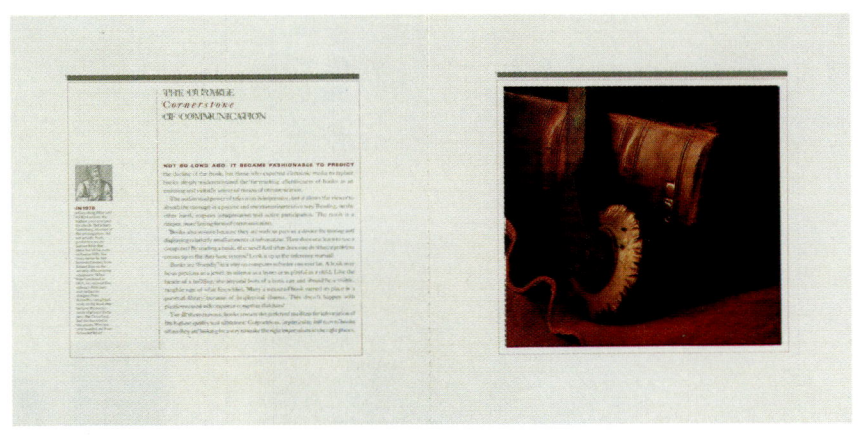

COMPLETE BOOK

AWARDED TO CREATIVE DIRECTORS
 Jim Ireland / Barbara Woolley
ART DIRECTORS / DESIGNERS
 Jim Ireland / Barbara Woolley
PHOTOGRAPHER
 Michael Kohn - Oyster Studio
PRINTER
 Ashton Potter
COLOUR SEPARATOR
 Passage Productions
CLIENT
 Corporate Books of Canada

MERIT

GRAPHIC DESIGN

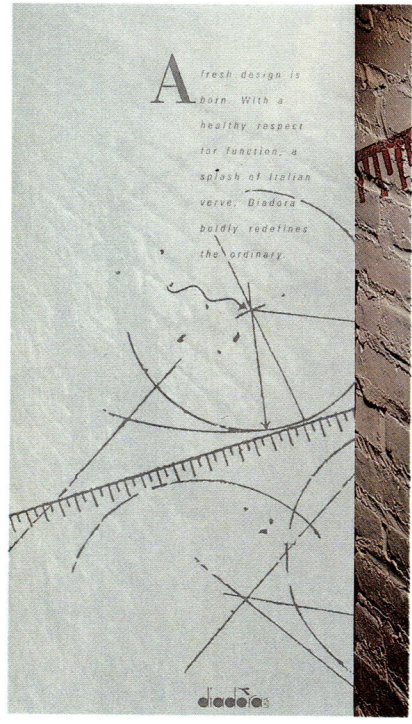
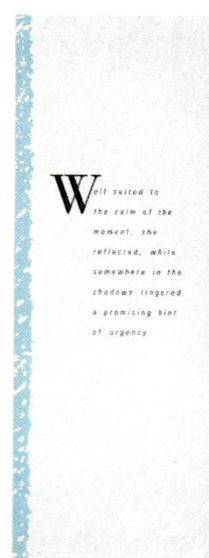

CATALOGUE

AWARDED TO
 Hornall Anderson Design Works
CREATIVE DIRECTOR / ART DIRECTOR
 Jack Anderson
DESIGNERS
 Jack Anderson / Cheri Huber
PHOTOGRAPHER
 Mark Burnside
ILLUSTRATOR
 Nancy Gellos
TYPOGRAPHER
 The Type Gallery
GRAPHIC DESIGN
 Hornall Anderson Design Works
CLIENT
 MacB Sports

CATALOGUE

AWARDED TO
 DesignSource / Telmet Design Associates
 Steven Evans / Ron Smith
DESIGNERS
 Richard Kerr / Nita Wallace
 Les Holloway
PHOTOGRAPHERS
 Steven Evans / Ron Smith
PRODUCTION STUDIO
 Telmet Design Associates
PRODUCTION SUPERVISOR
 Tiit Telmet
CLIENT
 Society of Graphic Designers of Canada

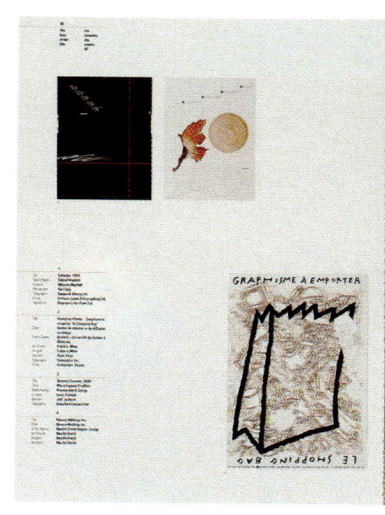
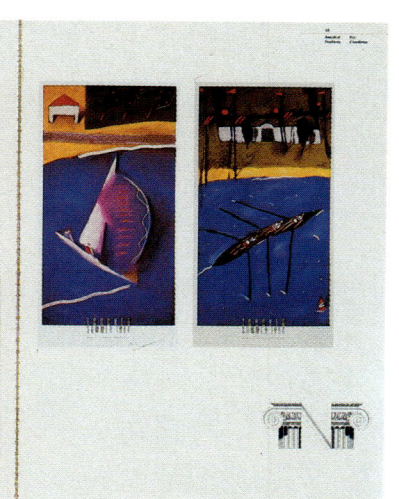

60 GRAPHIC EXCELLENCE

MERIT

GRAPHIC DESIGN

MAGAZINE COVER

AWARDED TO
 Conge Design
ART DIRECTOR
 Andy Kner
DESIGNER
 Bob Conge - Conge Design
ILLUSTRATOR
 Bob Conge
PRODUCTION STUDIO
 Conge Design
PUBLISHER
 RC Publications
CLIENT
 Print Magazine

CATALOGUE

AWARDED TO
 Charles Michael Helmken
CREATIVE DIRECTOR
 Charles Michael Helmken
ART DIRECTOR / DESIGNER
 Ikko Tanaka
PHOTOGRAPHER
 Tanaka Design Studio, Tokyo
EDITOR
 Charles Michael Helmken
PRINTER
 Dai-Nippon Printing Co. Ltd., Tokyo
PUBLISHER
 The Shoshin Society

GRAPHIC DESIGN 61

MERIT
GRAPHIC DESIGN

ADVERTISING POSTER

AWARDED TO
  Neville Smith
CREATIVE DIRECTOR / ART DIRECTOR
  Neville Smith
DESIGNER / TYPOGRAPHER
  Neville Smith
WRITER
  G.D.C. Ottawa Chapter
PRODUCTION STUDIO
  Neville Smith Graphic Design
PRINTER
  Arthurs-Jones Lithographing Ltd.
COLOUR SEPARATOR
  Herzig Somerville, Ltd.
CLIENT
  G.D.C. Ottawa Chapter

ADVERTISING POSTER

AWARDED TO
  Taylor & Browning Design Associates
ART DIRECTOR / DESIGNER
  Paul Browning
ILLUSTRATOR
  Gerard Gauci
TYPOGRAPHER
  Cooper & Beatty, Limited
PRINTER
  Arthurs-Jones Lithographing Limited
COLOUR SEPARATOR
  Empress Litho Plate
CLIENT
  Canadian Opera Company

MERIT

GRAPHIC DESIGN

ADVERTISING POSTER
AWARDED TO
　Don Weller
CREATIVE DIRECTOR / ART DIRECTOR
　Don Weller
DESIGNER
　Don Weller
PHOTOGRAPHER
　Stan Caplan
TYPOGRAPHER
　Alpha Graphix
WRITER
　Mikio Osaki
PRODUCTION STUDIO
　The Weller Institute for the Cure
　of Design, Inc.
PUBLISHER
　The Design Conference That Just Happens
　To Be In Park City 1980
CLIENT
　The Design Conference That Just Happens
　To Be In Park City 1980

ADVERTISING POSTER
AWARDED TO
　Ann Ames / Anita Kunz / George Kay
CREATIVE DIRECTOR / ART DIRECTOR
　Ann Ames
DESIGNER
　Ann Ames
ILLUSTRATOR
　Anita Kunz
TYPOGRAPHER
　George Kay
PRODUCTION STUDIO
　Ann Ames Design Associates Inc.
PRINTER
　Norgraphics Canada Limited
PUBLISHER
　Art Directors Club of Toronto
COLOUR SEPARATOR
　Batten Graphics
ADVERTISING AGENCY
　Ann Ames Design Associates Inc.
CLIENT
　Art Directors Club of Toronto

GRAPHIC DESIGN 63

MERIT

GRAPHIC DESIGN

POSTER

AWARDED TO
  Theo Dimson
CREATIVE DIRECTOR / ART DIRECTOR
  Theo Dimson
DESIGNER
  Theo Dimson
ILLUSTRATOR
  Theo Dimson / Ken Jackson
PRINTER
  Middleton Advertising
ADVERTISING AGENCY
  Theo Dimson Design Inc.
CLIENT
  TWP Theatre

ADVERTISING POSTER

AWARDED TO
  Frederic Metz / Alain Pilon
ART DIRECTOR / DESIGNER / WRITER
  Frederic Metz
ILLUSTRATOR / TYPOGRAPHER
  Alain Pilon / Compoplus Inc.
PRODUCTION STUDIO
  Bretelle – Uqam
PRINTER
  Atelier Des Sourds
CLIENT
  Centre de Creation et
  de Diffusion en Design

ADVERTISING POSTER

AWARDED TO
  Taylor & Browning Design Associates
ART DIRECTORS
  Michael Malloy / Scott Taylor
DESIGNER
  Diti Katona
PRINTER
  Arthurs-Jones Lithographing Ltd.
CLIENT
  Cadillac Fairview Shopping Centres

MERIT

GRAPHIC DESIGN

BIRTH ANNOUNCEMENT
AWARDED TO
  Hornall Anderson Design Works
CREATIVE DIRECTOR / ART DIRECTOR
  Jack Anderson
DESIGNER
  Jack Anderson
CALLIGRAPHY
  Bruce Hale
TYPOGRAPHER
  The Type Gallery
WRITER
  Steve Sandoz
PRINTER
  Zebra Press
GRAPHIC DESIGN
  Hornall Anderson Design Works
CLIENT
  Jack Anderson

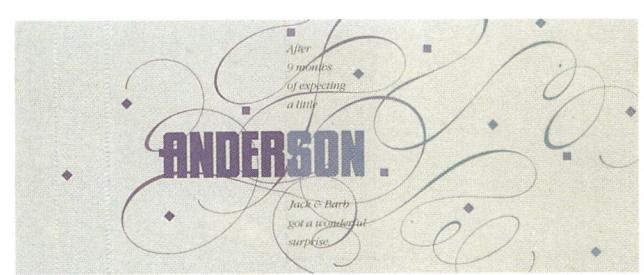

CHRISTMAS CARD
AWARDED TO
  Taylor & Browning Design Associates
ART DIRECTOR
  Scott Taylor
DESIGNERS
  Scott Taylor / John Pylypczak
ILLUSTRATORS
  Bill Boyko / Christine Bunn
  Barbara Klunder / Anita Kunz
  Des Montague
TYPOGRAPHER
  Word for Word Inc.
WRITER
  Scott Taylor
PRINTER
  Arthurs-Jones Lithographing Limited
CLIENT
  Cadillac Fairview Shopping Centres

PACKAGE DESIGN
AWARDED TO
  Ralph Colonna
DESIGNER
  Ralph Colonna
ILLUSTRATOR
  Bob Swartly
PRODUCTION STUDIO
  Colonna, Farrell Design
CLIENT
  Chateau Chevalier

OUTDOOR AD - TRANSIT
AWARDED TO
  Grant Tandy Ltd.
CREATIVE DIRECTOR
  David Adams
ART DIRECTOR
  Kieran McAuliffe
ILLUSTRATOR
  Thierry Thompson
TYPOGRAPHER
  Cooper & Beatty, Limited
ADVERTISING AGENCY
  Grant Tandy Ltd.

MERIT

GRAPHIC DESIGN

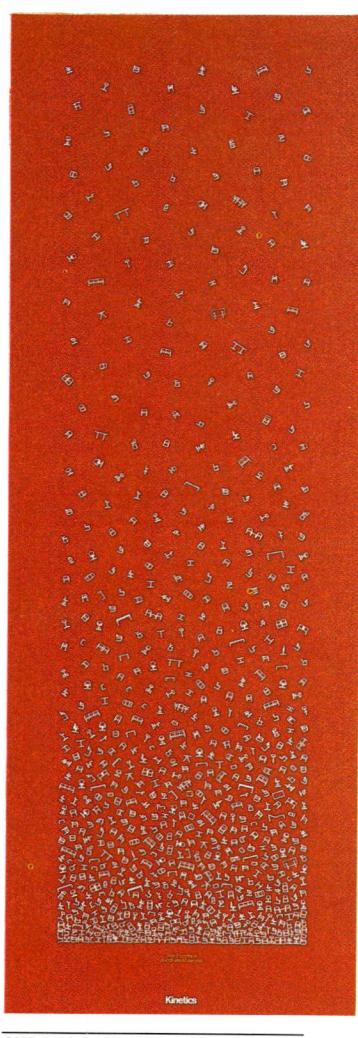

POSTAGE STAMPS
AWARDED TO
 Ernst Roch
CREATIVE DIRECTORS
 Ernst Roch / William Danard
ART DIRECTOR / DESIGNER
 Ernst Roch
ILLUSTRATOR
 Ernst Roch
PRINTER
 Ashton-Potter
CLIENT
 Canada Post Corporation

GREETING CARD
AWARDED TO
 Gottschalk & Ash International
DESIGNER
 Gottschalk & Ash International
PRINTER
 MacKinnon-Moncur Ltd.
CLIENT
 Gottschalk & Ash International

CHRISTMAS POSTER
AWARDED TO
 Taylor & Browning Design Associates
ART DIRECTOR
 Paul Browning
DESIGNER / ILLUSTRATOR
 Joe Drvaric
CLIENT
 Kinetics Furniture

INVITATION
AWARDED TO ART DIRECTOR Carmen Dunjko
ILLUSTRATORS Anita Kunz / Jeff Jackson
 Bill Frampton / Wendy Wortsman
 Nina Berkson / Kent Smith
CLIENT Creeds Ltd.

GRAPHIC EXCELLENCE

MERIT

GRAPHIC DESIGN

SELF PROMOTIONAL

AWARDED TO
 Huebner Kilvert Inc.
CREATIVE DIRECTORS
 Krista Huebner / David Kilvert
DESIGNER
 Krista Huebner

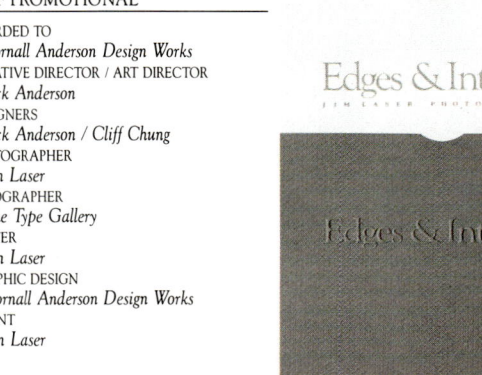

SELF PROMOTIONAL

AWARDED TO
 Hornall Anderson Design Works
CREATIVE DIRECTOR / ART DIRECTOR
 Jack Anderson
DESIGNERS
 Jack Anderson / Cliff Chung
PHOTOGRAPHER
 Jim Laser
TYPOGRAPHER
 The Type Gallery
WRITER
 Jim Laser
GRAPHIC DESIGN
 Hornall Anderson Design Works
CLIENT
 Jim Laser

SELF PROMOTIONAL

AWARDED TO
 Fernando Medina
CREATIVE DIRECTOR / ART DIRECTOR
 Fernando Medina
DESIGNER / ILLUSTRATOR
 Fernando Medina
PRODUCTION / PUBLISHER
 Medina Design

PROMOTIONAL

AWARDED TO
 Ernst Roch
CREATIVE DIRECTOR / ART DIRECTOR
 Ernst Roch
DESIGNER / ILLUSTRATOR
 Ernst Roch
PRODUCTION STUDIO
 Roch Design
CLIENT
 Museum of Modern Art

GRAPHIC DESIGN 67

CHAPTER 3
GRAPHIC EXCELLENCE

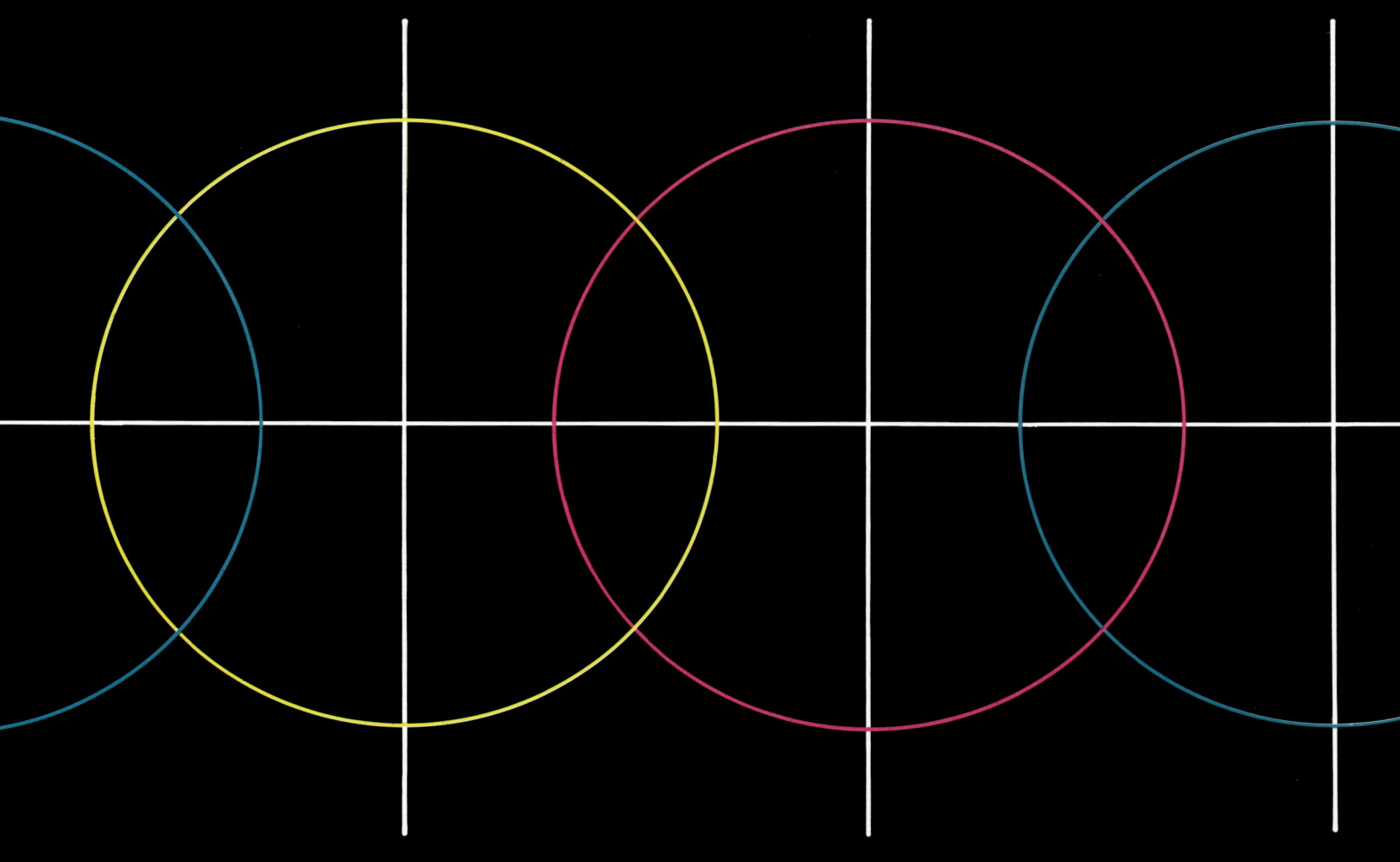

PHOTOGRAPHY

Submissions from photographers were from published and unpublished work, in categories which included annual report, brochure, self-promotional, outdoor advertising, complete book, P.O.P./exhibit/display, poster, magazine cover, and more.

Particularly interesting in their variety and creativity are the many self-promotional winners. The subject matter for these ranges from impressionistic still life to photos of food and elegant compositions of dinnerware and pasta. A wealth of ideas for self-promotion is offered here to the reader.

GOLD
PHOTOGRAPHY

SELF PROMOTIONAL

AWARDED TO
Joe Baraban
DESIGNER
Chris Hill
PHOTOGRAPHER
Joe Baraban
CLIENT
Olivet Group

PHOTOGRAPHY GOLD

FRAMING PRINTS

AWARDED TO
Chuck Rogers
PHOTOGRAPHER
Chuck Rogers

GOLD
PHOTOGRAPHY

COMPLETE BOOK

AWARDED TO
Robert Llewellyn
CREATIVE DIRECTOR / ART DIRECTOR
John Grant
PHOTOGRAPHER
Robert Llewellyn
PRINTER
Stephenson Inc.
PUBLISHER / CLIENT
Thomasson-Grant Publishing Inc.

SILVER
PHOTOGRAPHY

ANNUAL REPORT

AWARDED TO
 Joe Baraban
DESIGNER
 Woody Pirtle
PHOTOGRAPHER
 Joe Baraban
CLIENT
 Lomas & Nettleton

ANNUAL REPORT

AWARDED TO
 Camille Vickers
ART DIRECTOR
 Stephan Geissbuhler
DESIGNER
 Chermayeff and Geismar
PHOTOGRAPHER
 Camille Vickers
PRINTER
 Sanders Printing Co.
CLIENT
 Thyssen Bornemisza 1977 AR

SILVER
PHOTOGRAPHY

BROCHURE

AWARDED TO
 Craig Wells
ART DIRECTOR
 Brad Ghormley
DESIGNER
 Steve Smit
PHOTOGRAPHER
 Craig Wells
CLIENT
 Noel Plastering & Stucco, Inc.

OUTDOOR ADVERTISING

AWARDED TO
 Yuri Dojc
ART DIRECTOR
 Stuart Hood
PHOTOGRAPHER
 Yuri Dojc
PHOTO ASSISTANT
 Craig Hyde Parker
MODEL
 Kelly Craig
ADVERTISING AGENCY
 Vickers & Benson
CLIENT
 Brooks

SILVER

PHOTOGRAPHY

SELF PROMOTIONAL

AWARDED TO
Brett Froomer
PHOTOGRAPHER
Brett Froomer
PRINTER
Elliot Graphics

CALENDAR

AWARDED TO
Yuri Dojc
DESIGNER
Eskind Waddell
PHOTOGRAPHER
Yuri Dojc
TYPOGRAPHER
Cooper & Beatty
PRINTER
Arthurs-Jones Lithographing, Ltd.
COLOUR SEPARATOR
Empress Litho

MERIT
PHOTOGRAPHY

CONSUMER MAGAZINE AD

AWARDED TO
  Larry Williams
ART DIRECTOR
  Terry Tomalty
PHOTOGRAPHER
  Larry Williams
ADVERTISING AGENCY
  J. Walter Thompson Company Ltd.
CLIENT
  Kraft & Christie

CONSUMER MAGAZINE AD

AWARDED TO
  Theo Dimson
CREATIVE DIRECTOR / ART DIRECTOR
  Theo Dimson
DESIGNER
  Theo Dimson
PHOTOGRAPHER
  Shin Sugino
COLOUR SEPARATOR
  Herzig Somerville, Ltd.
ADVERTISING AGENCY
  Theo Dimson Design Inc.
CLIENT
  Liptons Fashion Wear Limited

MERIT

PHOTOGRAPHY

CONSUMER MAGAZINE AD - SERIES
AWARDED TO
 Larry Williams
ART DIRECTOR
 Paul Lavoie
PHOTOGRAPHER
 Larry Williams
ADVERTISING AGENCY
 J. Walter Thompson Company Ltd.
CLIENT
 Kraft

MERIT
PHOTOGRAPHY

TRADE ADVERTISEMENT

AWARDED TO
 Joe Baraban
DESIGNER
 Scott Schelstrom
PHOTOGRAPHER
 Joe Baraban
ADVERTISING AGENCY
 Needham, Harper
CLIENT
 Sesame Park

TRADE ADVERTISEMENT

AWARDED TO
 Philip Rostron
ART DIRECTORS
 Jon Vopni / Sandra Parsons
PHOTOGRAPHER
 Philip Rostron / Instil Productions
ADVERTISING AGENCY
 Vopni & Parsons Design
CLIENT
 Provincial Papers

78 GRAPHIC EXCELLENCE

MERIT
PHOTOGRAPHY

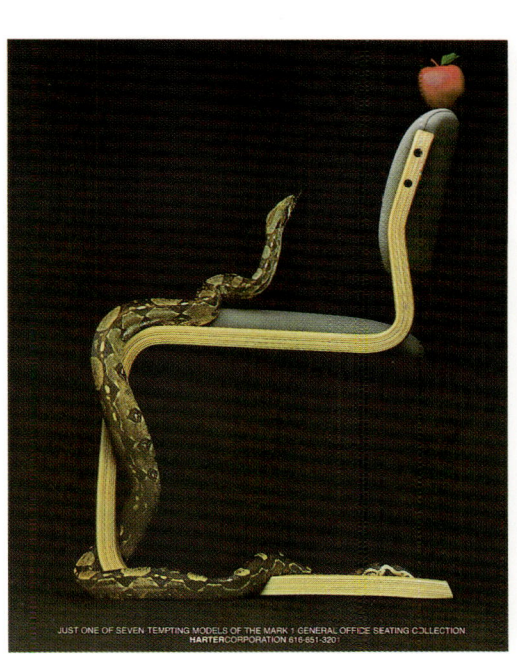

TRADE ADVERTISEMENT - SERIES
AWARDED TO
Bender & Bender Photography
CREATIVE DIRECTOR
Bob Bender
ART DIRECTOR
Doug Fisher
ADVERTISING AGENCY
Lord, Sullivan & Yoder
CLIENT
Harter Corporation

MERIT
PHOTOGRAPHY

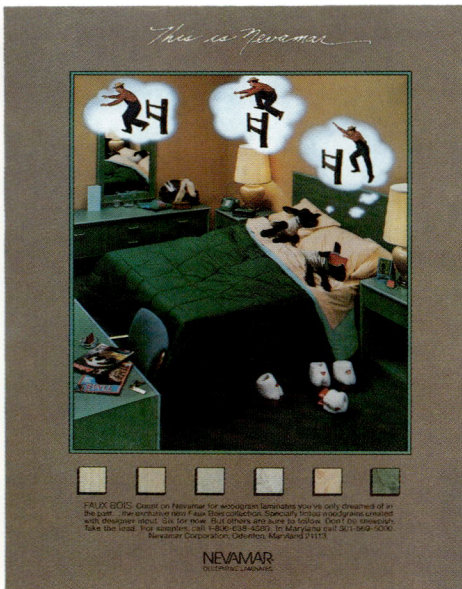

TRADE ADVERTISEMENT - SERIES

AWARDED TO
Bender & Bender Photography
CREATIVE DIRECTOR
Bob Bender
ART DIRECTOR
Doug Fisher
PHOTOGRAPHER
Fred Bender
ADVERTISING AGENCY
Lord, Sullivan & Yoder
CLIENT
Nevamar Corporation

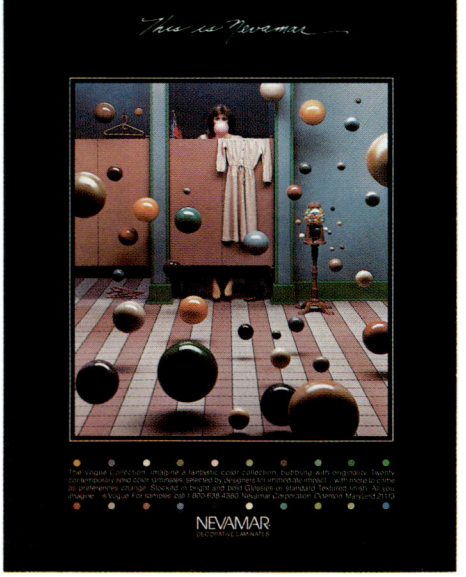

MERIT
PHOTOGRAPHY

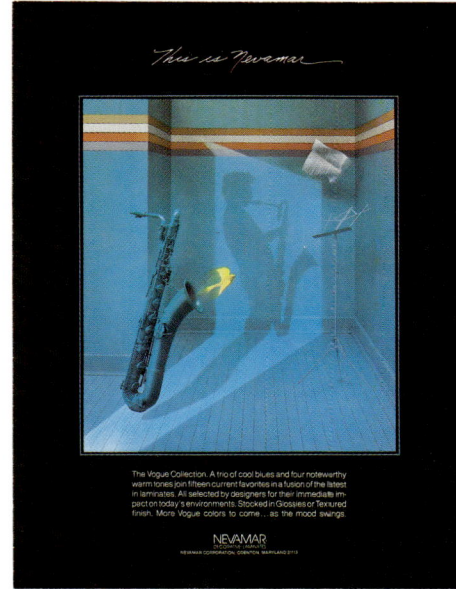

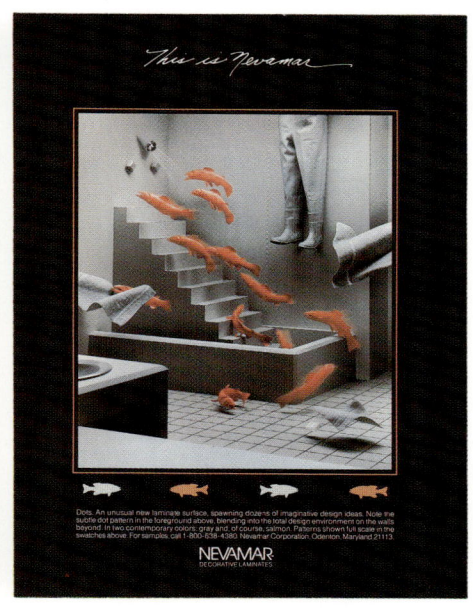
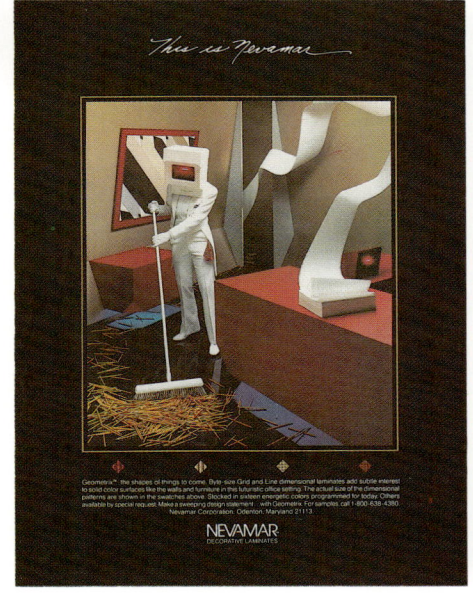

PHOTOGRAPHY 81

MERIT
PHOTOGRAPHY

ANNUAL REPORT

AWARDED TO
Joe Baraban
DESIGNER
Lowell Williams
PHOTOGRAPHER
Joe Baraban
CLIENT
Oil Tools International

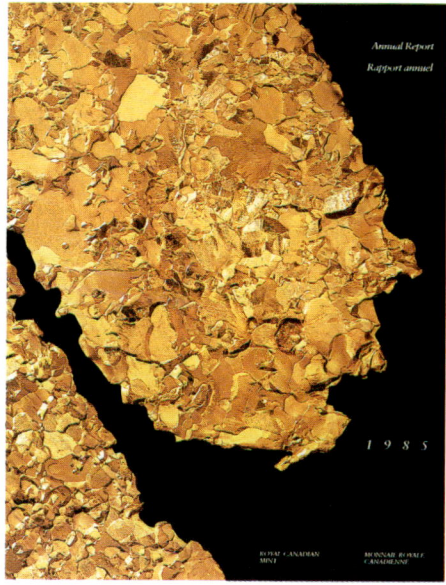

ANNUAL REPORT

AWARDED TO
The Davidson Bénard Group / Furman Graphic Design
DESIGNER
Aviva Furman
PHOTOGRAPHERS
Robert Davidson / Joël Bénard
CLIENT
The Royal Canadian Mint

MERIT

PHOTOGRAPHY

COMPLETE BOOK
AWARDED TO
  Peter Christopher
ART DIRECTOR
  Robert Hyland
DESIGNERS
  Jon Vopni / Robert Hyland
PHOTOGRAPHER
  Peter Christopher
ILLUSTRATORS
  Jon Vopni / George Kay
  Larry Bloss / Frank Bonigut
  Al Ebsen
DESIGN FIRM
  Robert Hyland Design & Associates
CLIENT
  M.C. Charters & Co. Ltd.

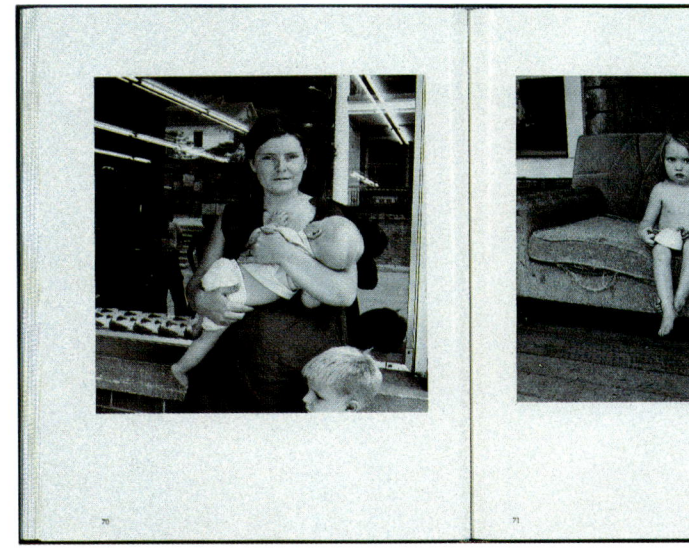

COMPLETE BOOK
AWARDED TO PHOTOGRAPHER
  Milton Rogovin
ART DIRECTOR / DESIGNER
  Audrey Meyer
PRINTER
  Toppan Printing Co.
PUBLISHER
  University of Washington

MERIT
PHOTOGRAPHY

ADVERTISING POSTER

AWARDED TO
 Ron Baxter Smith
ART DIRECTOR / DESIGNER
 Del Terrelonge
PHOTOGRAPHER
 Ron Baxter Smith
TYPOGRAPHER
 Karen Cheeseman / Hunter Brown
WRITER
 Paul Bailey
PRODUCTION STUDIO
 Continental Bank Studio
PRINTER
 Arthurs-Jones Lithographing Ltd.
COLOUR SEPARATOR
 Acme Graphics Ltd.
CLIENT
 Continental Bank of Canada

COMPLETE BOOK

AWARDED TO
 Michael Kohn - Oyster Studio
CREATIVE DIRECTORS
 Jim Ireland / Barbara Woolley
ART DIRECTORS
 Jim Ireland / Barbara Woolley
DESIGNERS
 Jim Ireland / Barbara Woolley
PHOTOGRAPHER
 Michael Kohn - Oyster Studio
PRINTER
 Ashton Potter
COLOUR SEPARATOR
 Passage Productions
CLIENT
 Corporate Books of Canada

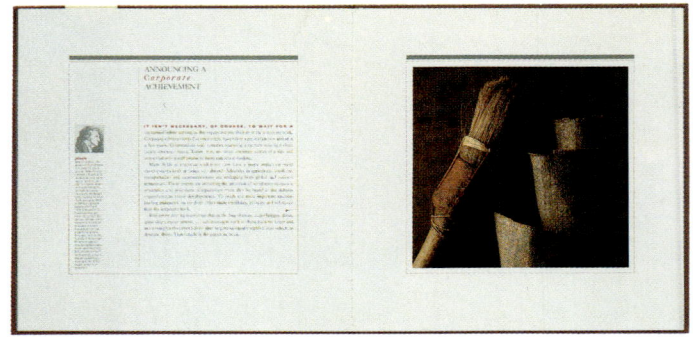

84 GRAPHIC EXCELLENCE

MERIT

PHOTOGRAPHY

P.O.P. / EXHIBIT / DISPLAY

AWARDED TO
 Richard Saint John
ART DIRECTOR
 Richard Saint John
PHOTOGRAPHER
 Richard Saint John
CLIENT
 Bell Canada

OUTDOOR ADVERTISING

AWARDED TO
 Ivor Sharp
CREATIVE DIRECTOR
 Graham Watt
ART DIRECTOR / DESIGNER
 Jim Burt
PHOTOGRAPHER
 Ivor Sharp
MODEL
 Harriet England
TYPOGRAPHER
 Typecraft
WRITER
 Graham Watt
ADVERTISING AGENCY
 McKim / Watt Burt
CLIENT
 Ontario Milk Marketing Board

PHOTOGRAPHY 85

MERIT

PHOTOGRAPHY

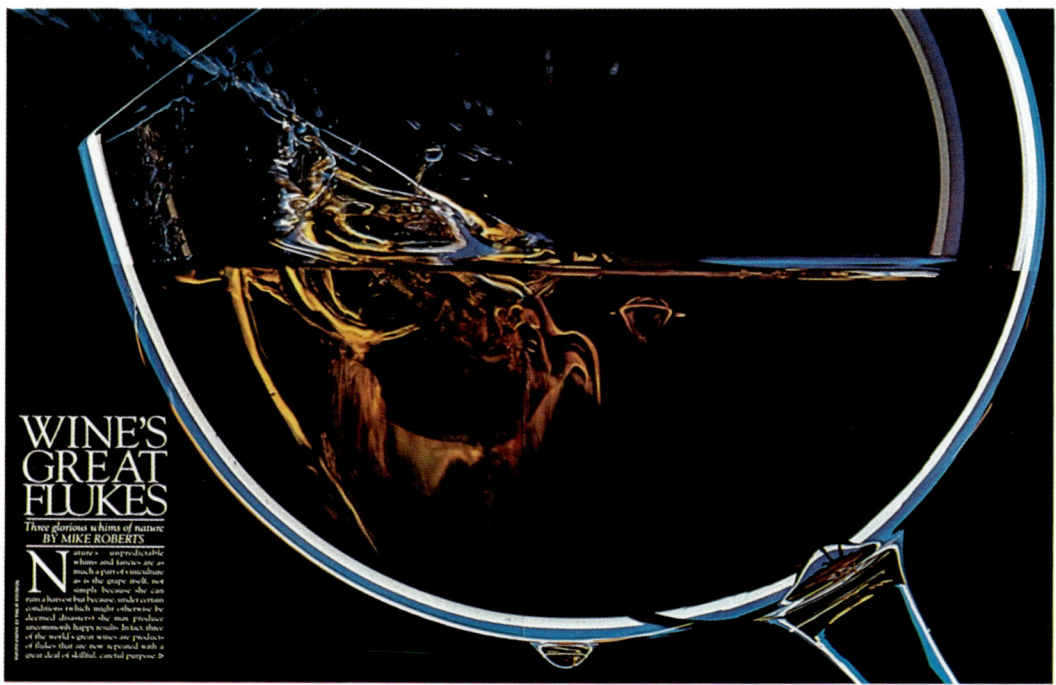

EDITORIAL SPREAD

AWARDED TO
Philip Rostron
ART DIRECTOR
John Eby
PHOTOGRAPHER
Philip Rostron / Instil Productions
CLIENT
Epicure

EDITORIAL SPREAD

AWARDED TO
Ron Levine
PHOTOGRAPHER
Ron Levine
PHOTO ASSISTANT
Darrell Rex
WRITER
Nancy Southam
EDITOR
Kevin McKeown
PUBLISHER
Montreal Magazines Inc.
CLIENT
Montreal Magazine

MERIT

PHOTOGRAPHY

MAGAZINE COVER

AWARDED TO
 Montreal Ce Mois-Ci
ART DIRECTOR
 Marie-José Chagnon
PHOTOGRAPHER
 Monic Richard
PHOTO ASSISTANT
 Francis Tremblay
MODEL
 Marianne Porter
TYPOGRAPHER
 Typo Express
EDITOR
 André Ducharme
PUBLISHER
 Les Magazines Montreal Inc.

MAGAZINE COVER

AWARDED TO
 George Dunbar
PHOTOGRAPHER
 George Dunbar
EDITOR
 James R. Cypher
PUBLISHER
 IBM World Trade Corp. (USA)
CLIENT
 IBM Canada Ltd.

MERIT
PHOTOGRAPHY

SELF PROMOTIONAL - SERIES
AWARDED TO
Les Szurkowski
PHOTOGRAPHER
Les Szurkowski

FRAMING PRINT
AWARDED TO
Les Szurkowski
PHOTOGRAPHER
Les Szurkowski

MERIT

PHOTOGRAPHY

POSTER
AWARDED TO
 Matthew Wiley
ART DIRECTORS
 Bob Russell / Stan Olthius
DESIGNER
 Bob Russell -
 Carverhill, Russell & Timmerman
PHOTOGRAPHER
 Matthew Wiley
PHOTO ASSISTANT
 Altman
MODEL
 Zoey (legs) / Dick (Duck)
PRINTER
 Proving Specialities Ltd.
COLOUR SEPARATOR
 Passage Productions Inc.
CLIENT
 Boardwork / Sharpshooter

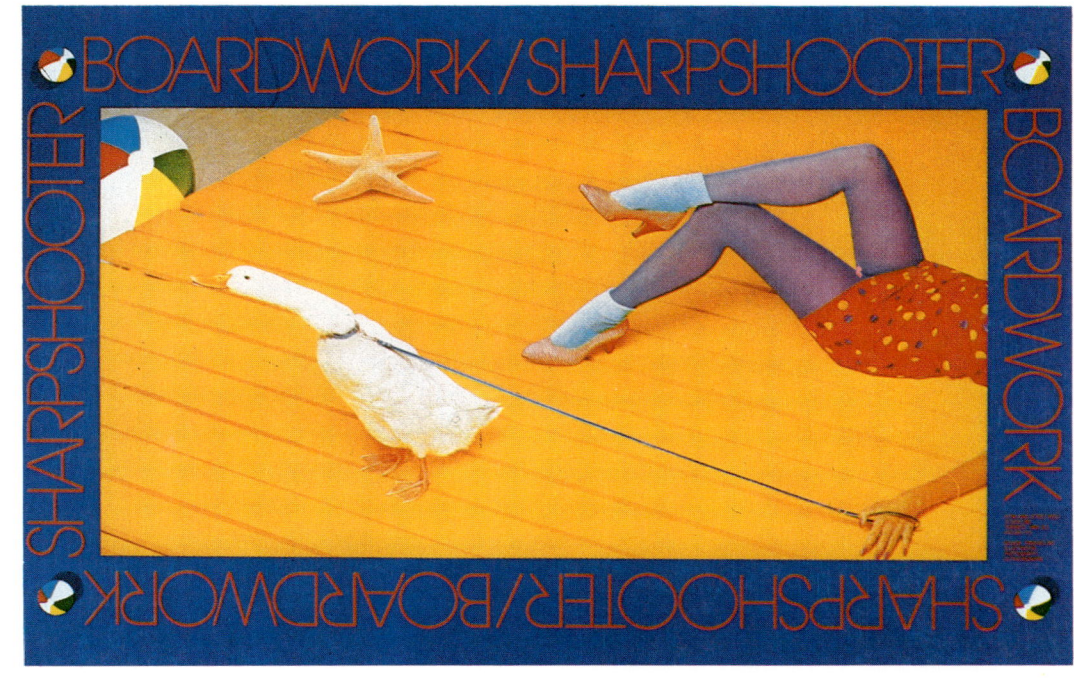

CALENDAR
AWARDED TO PHOTOGRAPHER
 Lonnie Duka
CREATIVE DIRECTOR
 Lonnie Duka
DESIGNER / PRODUCTION SUPERVISOR
 Steve Tucker
WRITER / EDITOR
 Susan Lane
PRODUCTION STUDIO
 Asbury Tucker
PRINTER
 Anderson
PUBLISHER / CLIENT
 Fluor Corporation

CALENDAR
AWARDED TO PHOTOGRAPHER
 Lonnie Duka
CREATIVE DIRECTOR
 Lonnie Duka
DESIGNER / PRODUCTION SUPERVISOR
 Steve Tucker
WRITER / EDITOR
 Susan Lane
PRODUCTION STUDIO
 Asbury Tucker
PRINTER
 George Rice & Sons
PUBLISHER / CLIENT
 Fluor Corporation

MERIT
PHOTOGRAPHY

SELF PROMOTIONAL

AWARDED TO
  Struan Campbell-Smith
CREATIVE DIRECTOR / PHOTOGRAPHER
  Struan Campbell-Smith
PHOTO ASSISTANT
  Michael Lee
MODEL
  Leslie Prowse
LOCATION
  Dubrovnik, Yugoslavia
MAKE-UP
  Steve Marino
HAIR
  Ian Djurkin
PUBLISHER
  Creative Source

SELF PROMOTIONAL

AWARDED TO
  Mark Tomalty
PHOTOGRAPHER
  Mark Tomalty

MERIT

PHOTOGRAPHY

SELF PROMOTIONAL
AWARDED TO
 Garry Kan
PHOTOGRAPHER
 Garry Kan

SELF PROMOTIONAL
AWARDED TO
 Mason Morfit
CREATIVE DIRECTOR / ART DIRECTOR
 Mason Morfit
DESIGNER / PHOTOGRAPHER
 Mason Morfit
TYPOGRAPHER
 Frank's Type
WRITER
 Mason Morfit
PRINTER / COLOUR SEPARATOR
 Hennegan Co.

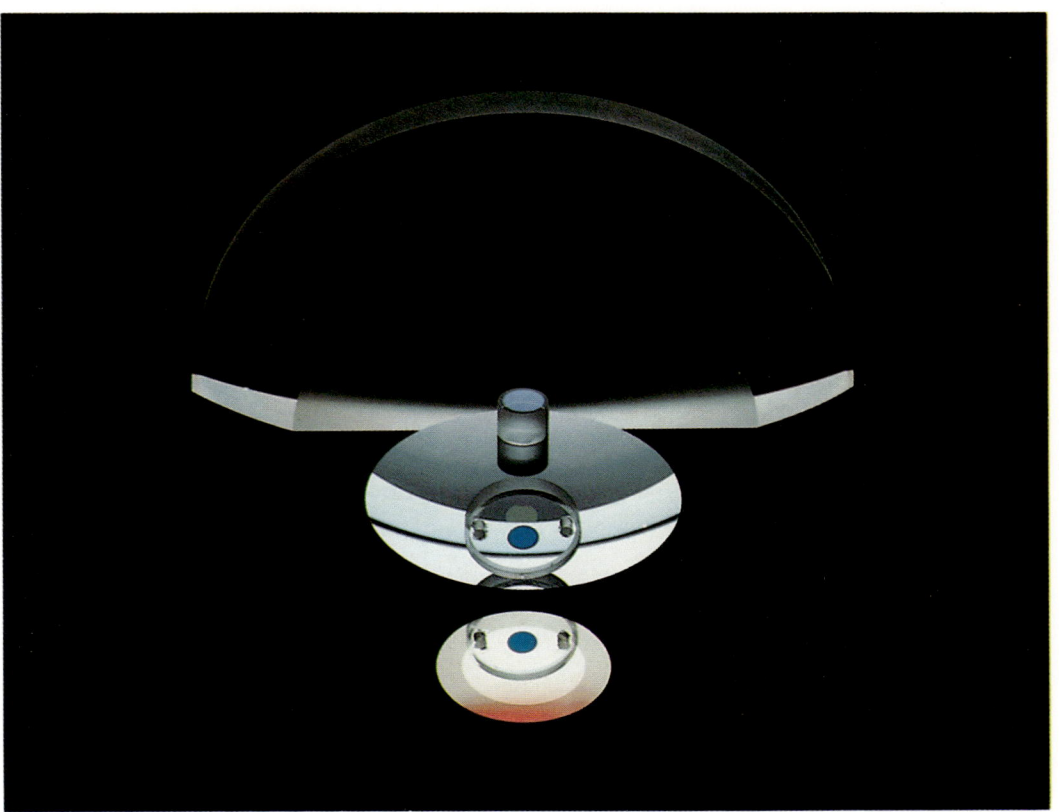

MERIT
PHOTOGRAPHY

SELF PROMOTIONAL - SERIES
AWARDED TO
Joe Baraban
DESIGNER
Bill Carson
PHOTOGRAPHER
Joe Baraban

MERIT

PHOTOGRAPHY

SELF PROMOTIONAL

AWARDED TO
 Sam Errico
ART DIRECTOR
 Sam Errico
DESIGNERS
 Javier / Tsang
PHOTOGRAPHER
 Sam Errico
PRINTER
 Cannon Press
CLIENT
 Errico Photography

SELF PROMOTIONAL

AWARDED TO
 Carol Kaplan
DESIGNER
 Vic Cevoli
PHOTOGRAPHER
 Carol Kaplan
STYLIST
 Jeffrey Katz

PHOTOGRAPHY 93

CHAPTER 4

GRAPHIC EXCELLENCE

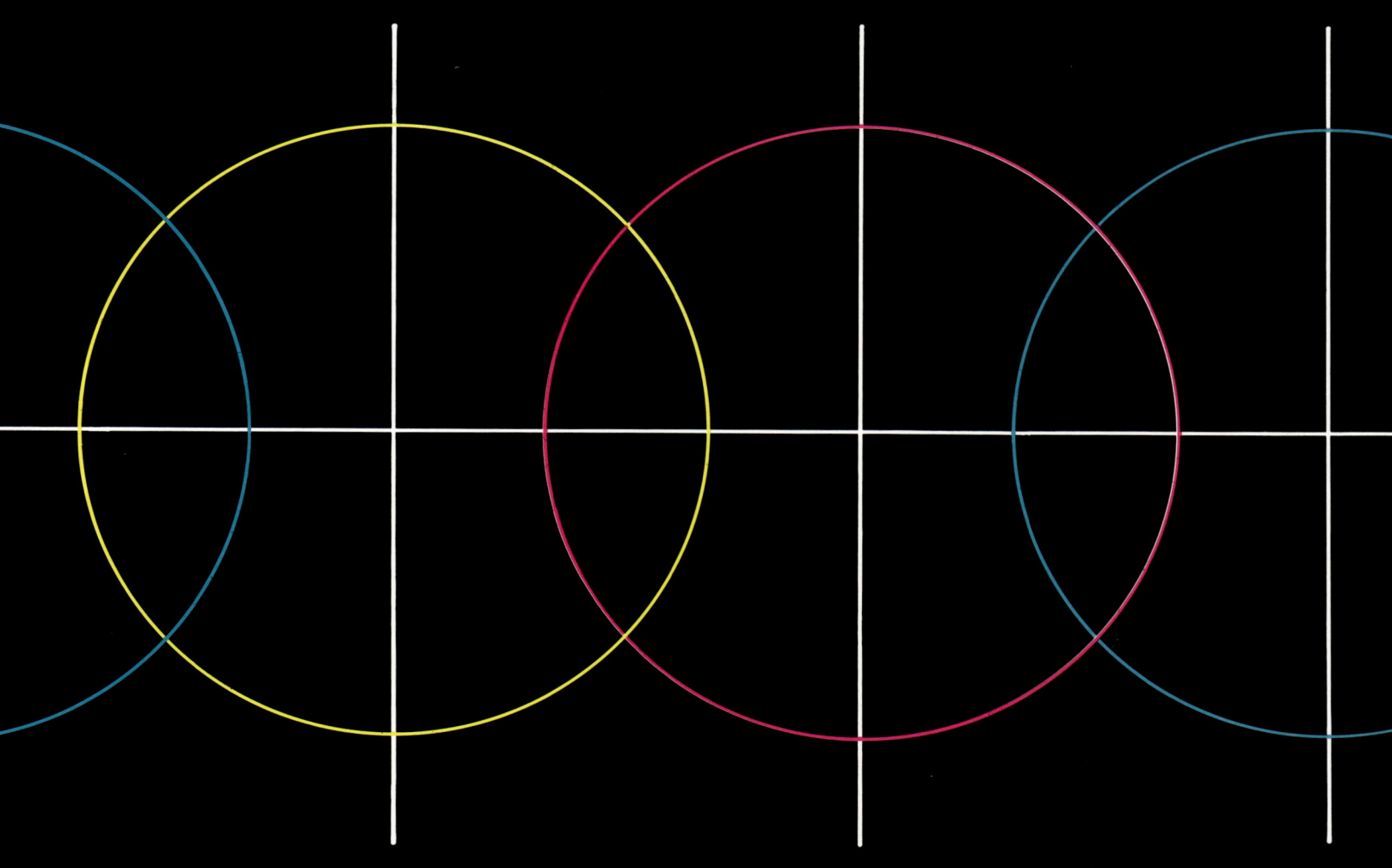

ILLUSTRATION

Award winners in this category were selected from entries of published and unpublished work. Winning illustrations are witty, whimsical, thought-provoking, frightening, and simply pretty to look at. Classifications include magazine cover, complete children's book, editorial page, consumer magazine cover, book cover, greeting card, and others.

Among media used are airbrush, watercolor, oil and poster paint, pastel, ink-blotting, plus line-drawing, collage, and mixed media. The range of subject matter and artistry makes this a compelling chapter.

GOLD
ILLUSTRATION

ADVERTISING POSTER
AWARDED TO
 Stéphan Daigle
CREATIVE DIRECTOR / ILLUSTRATOR
 Stéphan Daigle
ART DIRECTOR / DESIGNER
 Gianni Caccia
TYPOGRAPHER
 Composition Solidaire
PRINTER
 Express Art

GOLD

ILLUSTRATION

POSTER
AWARDED TO
J. Rafal Olbinski
ART DIRECTOR / DESIGNER
J. Rafal Olbinski
ILLUSTRATOR
J. Rafal Olbinski
PUBLISHER
Papermania Studio
CLIENT
Daytop

SILVER
ILLUSTRATION

EDITORIAL PAGES - SERIES
AWARDED TO
  Normand Cousineau
CREATIVE DIRECTOR
  Normand Cousineau
ART DIRECTOR / DESIGNER
  Gianni Caccia
ILLUSTRATOR
  Normand Cousineau
PRINTER
  Payette et Simms
CLIENT
  Les Éditions Vice Versa

SILVER

ILLUSTRATION

MAGAZINE COVER

AWARDED TO
 Daniel Sylvestre
CREATIVE DIRECTOR / ILLUSTRATOR
 Daniel Sylvestre
ART DIRECTOR / DESIGNER
 Gianni Caccia
PRINTER
 Payette et Simms
COLOUR SEPARATOR
 Allard Studio
CLIENT
 Les Éditions Vice Versa

COMPLETE CHILDREN'S BOOK

AWARDED TO
 Tundra Books Inc.
CREATIVE DIRECTOR / ART DIRECTOR
 May Cutler
DESIGNER
 Dan O'Leary
ILLUSTRATOR / WRITER
 Lindee Climo
PRINTER
 Pierre Des Marais
PUBLISHER
 Tundra Books Inc.
COLOUR SEPARATOR
 John Weatherhill

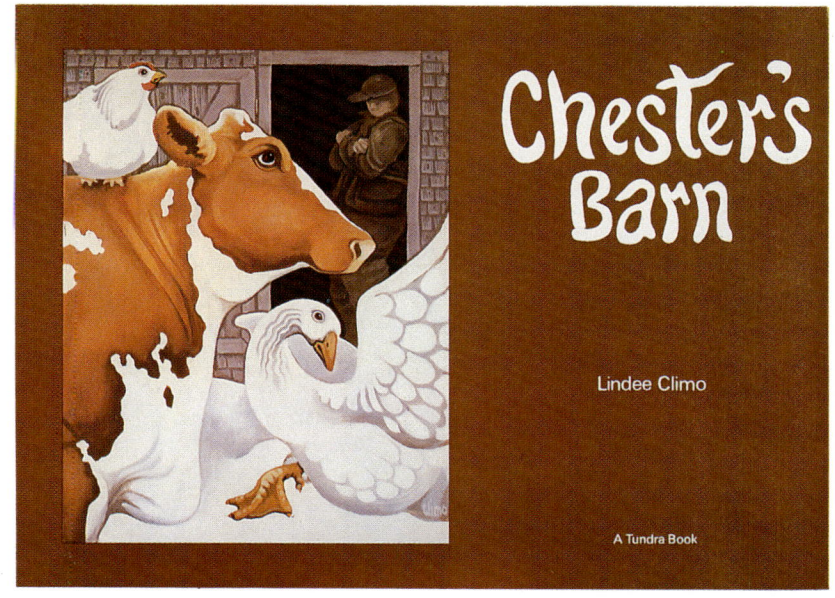

ILLUSTRATION 99

MERIT
ILLUSTRATION

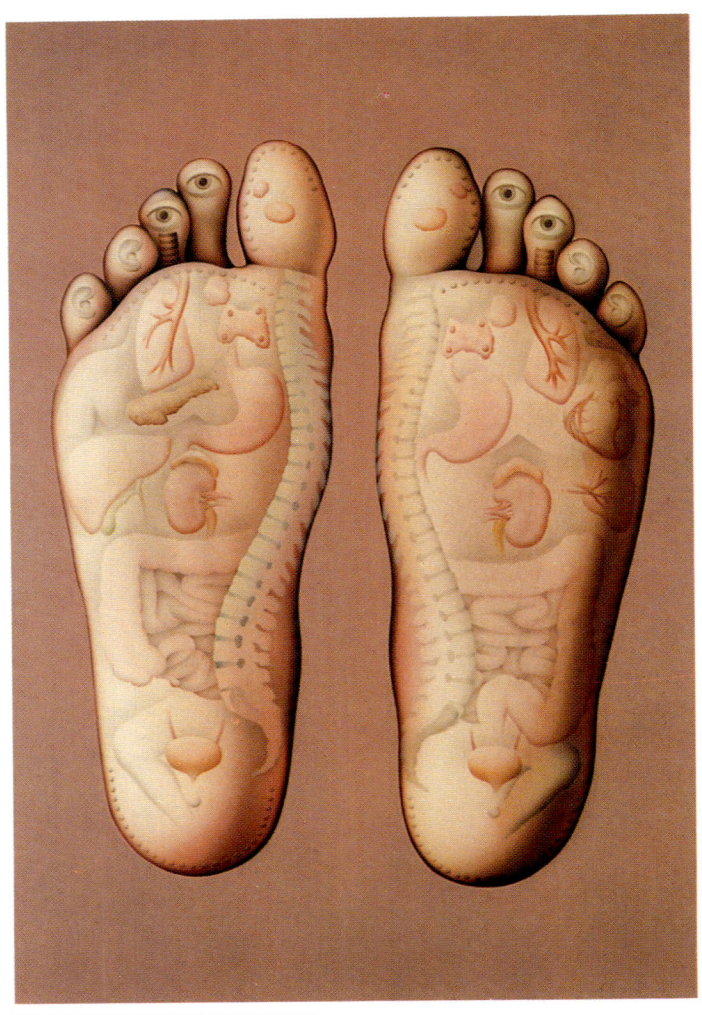

TRADE ADVERTISEMENT

AWARDED TO
  Leonard E. Morgan
ART DIRECTOR
  Michael V. Phillips
ILLUSTRATOR
  Leonard E. Morgan
ADVERTISING AGENCY
  Frank J. Corbett, Inc.
CLIENT
  Westwood Pharmaceuticals

CONSUMER MAGAZINE AD

AWARDED TO
  Bill Davis
ART DIRECTOR
  David Bryer
DESIGNER / ILLUSTRATOR
  Bill Davis
PUBLISHER
  Children's TV Workshop
CLIENT
  Electric Co. Magazine

MERIT

ILLUSTRATION

ANNUAL REPORT
AWARDED TO
 Julius Ciss
ART DIRECTOR
 Brian Richards
ILLUSTRATOR
 Julius Ciss
ADVERTISING AGENCY
 Karnak Inc.
CLIENT
 Redpath Industries

COMPLETE CHILDREN'S BOOK
AWARDED TO
 Barbara Reid
ART DIRECTOR
 Kathryn Cole
PHOTOGRAPHER
 Ian Crysler
ILLUSTRATOR
 Barbara Reid
PUBLISHER
 Scholastic-Tab Publications

ILLUSTRATION 101

MERIT
ILLUSTRATION

COMPLETE CHILDREN'S BOOK

AWARDED TO ILLUSTRATOR
 Michèle Lemieux
DESIGNER
 Sylvia Frezzolini
ART DIRECTOR
 Gisela Stottele
WRITER
 Evelyne Hasler
PUBLISHER
 William Morrow & Co.

COMPLETE CHILDREN'S BOOK

AWARDED TO
 Tundra Books Inc.
CREATIVE DIRECTOR / ART DIRECTOR
 May Cutler
DESIGNER
 Michael Cutler
PHOTOGRAPHER
 A. Kilbertus
ILLUSTRATOR / WRITER
 Stéphane Poulin
PUBLISHER
 Tundra Books Inc.

MERIT

ILLUSTRATION

BOOK COVER
AWARDED TO
 Holt, Rinehart and Winston of Canada
ART DIRECTOR
 Mary Opper
DESIGNER
 Martin Gould
ILLUSTRATOR
 Doug Martin
PUBLISHER
 Holt, Rinehart and Winston of Canada
COLOUR SEPARATOR
 Bergman Graphics
CLIENT
 Holt, Rinehart and Winston

ALBUM COVER
AWARDED TO
 Victoria Birta
ART DIRECTOR
 Zoltan Birta
DESIGNER / ILLUSTRATOR
 Victoria Birta
CLIENT
 Charles Amore &
 The Twelfth Fret Publishing

MERIT
ILLUSTRATION

BOOK ILLUSTRATION

AWARDED TO ILLUSTRATOR
Tadami Yamada
CREATIVE DIRECTOR
Kazui Kawakami
ART DIRECTORS
Tadami Yamada / Hidetaka Mochizuki
DESIGNER
Katuto Mochizuki - Hot Art
PRODUCTION STUDIO
Shinshusha
PRINTER / COLOUR SEPARATOR
Dai Nippon Printing Co. Ltd.
PUBLISHER / CLIENT
Gakken

BOOK ILLUSTRATION

AWARDED TO
Holt, Rinehart and Winston of Canada
ART DIRECTOR
Mary Opper
DESIGNER
Martin Gould
ILLUSTRATOR
Rene Zamic
PUBLISHER / CLIENT
Holt, Rinehart and Winston of Canada
COLOUR SEPARATOR
Bergman Graphics

104 GRAPHIC EXCELLENCE

MERIT

ILLUSTRATION

BOOK ILLUSTRATION
AWARDED TO
  Holt, Rinehart and Winston of Canada
ART DIRECTOR
  Mary Opper
DESIGNER
  Martin Gould
ILLUSTRATOR
  Wojtek Gorczynski
PUBLISHER
  Holt, Rinehart and Winston of Canada

MAGAZINE SPOT - BLACK & WHITE
AWARDED TO
  Daniel Sylvestre
CREATIVE DIRECTOR
  Daniel Sylvestre
ART DIRECTOR / DESIGNER
  Gianni Caccia
ILLUSTRATOR
  Daniel Sylvestre
PRINTER
  Payette et Simms
CLIENT
  Les Éditions Vice Versa

ILLUSTRATION 105

MERIT
ILLUSTRATION

MAGAZINE COVER

AWARDED TO
  Montreal ce mois-ci
CREATIVE DIRECTOR
  Jocelyne Fournel
ILLUSTRATOR
  Yvan Adam
EDITOR
  André Ducharme
PRINTER
  Ronalds Federated
PUBLISHER
  Les Magazines Montreal Inc.
COLOUR SEPARATOR
  H.I. Graphics

BOOK COVER

AWARDED TO
  Montreal Magazine
ART DIRECTOR
  Hamo Habdalian
ILLUSTRATOR
  Mireille Levert
TYPOGRAPHER
  Adcomp
EDITOR
  Kevin McKeown
PRINTER
  Ronalds Federated
COLOUR SEPARATOR
  H.I. Graphics
CLIENT
  Montreal Magazine

MERIT

ILLUSTRATION

MAGAZINE COVER

AWARDED TO
  Linda Scharf
ART DIRECTOR
  Robert Birnbaum
DESIGNER / ILLUSTRATOR
  Linda Scharf
PRINTER
  Charles River Publishing
PUBLISHER / CLIENT
  Stuff Magazine

MAGAZINE COVER

AWARDED TO
  Mireille Levert
ART DIRECTOR / DESIGNER
  Hamo Habdalian
ILLUSTRATOR
  Mireille Levert
EDITOR
  Kevin Dale McKeown
CLIENT
  Montreal Magazine

MERIT
ILLUSTRATION

MAGAZINE COVER

AWARDED TO
 Julius Ciss
ART DIRECTOR
 Nick Burnett
ILLUSTRATOR
 Julius Ciss
PUBLISHER
 Macleans Magazine

MAGAZINE COVER

AWARDED TO
 Cliff Sloan
ART DIRECTOR / DESIGNER
 Cliff Sloan
ILLUSTRATOR
 Robin Morris
PRODUCTION STUDIO
 SloanArt Inc.
PUBLISHER
 Rave Communications
CLIENT
 Radio City Music Hall

108 GRAPHIC EXCELLENCE

MERIT

ILLUSTRATION

MAGAZINE COVER

AWARDED TO
 Normand Cousineau
CREATIVE DIRECTOR
 Normand Cousineau
ART DIRECTOR / DESIGNER
 Gianni Caccia
ILLUSTRATOR
 Normand Cousineau
CLIENT
 Les Éditions Vice Versa

MAGAZINE COVER

AWARDED TO
 Julius Ciss
ART DIRECTOR
 James Lawrence
ILLUSTRATOR
 Julius Ciss
PUBLISHER
 Harrowsmith Magazine

MERIT
ILLUSTRATION

EDITORIAL PAGE

AWARDED TO
Julius Ciss
ART DIRECTOR
Steve Manley
ILLUSTRATOR
Julius Ciss
PUBLISHER
Canadian Business Magazine

EDITORIAL PAGE

AWARDED TO
Julius Ciss
ART DIRECTOR
Jon Eby
ILLUSTRATOR
Julius Ciss
PUBLISHER
Quest Magazine

110 GRAPHIC EXCELLENCE

MERIT

ILLUSTRATION

EDITORIAL PAGE
AWARDED TO
Julius Ciss
ART DIRECTOR
Ken Rodmell
ILLUSTRATOR
Julius Ciss
PUBLISHER
Toronto Life

EDITORIAL PAGE
AWARDED TO
Julius Ciss
ART DIRECTOR
Jon Eby
ILLUSTRATOR
Julius Ciss
PUBLISHER
Quest Magazine

ILLUSTRATION 111

MERIT
ILLUSTRATION

EDITORIAL PAGE
AWARDED TO
 Julius Ciss
ART DIRECTOR
 Ursula Kaiser
ILLUSTRATOR
 Julius Ciss
PUBLISHER
 Madame au Foyer Magazine

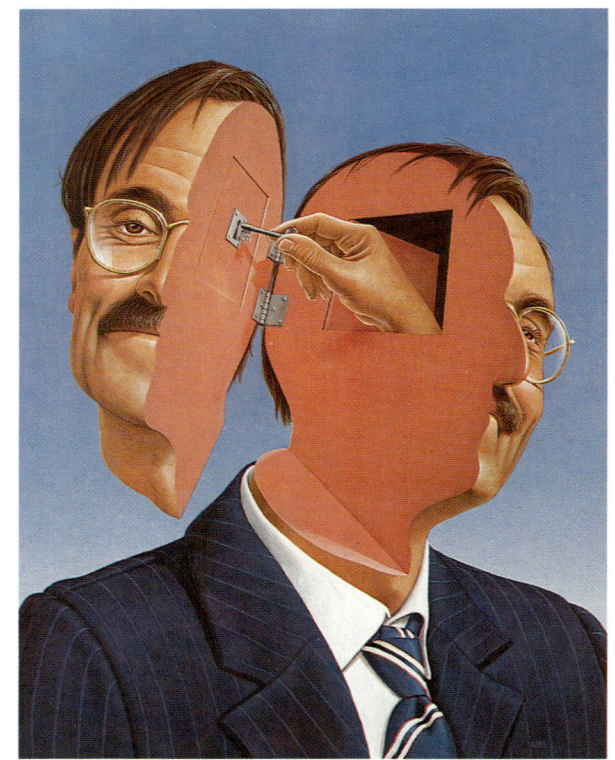

EDITORIAL PAGE
AWARDED TO
 Julius Ciss
ART DIRECTOR
 Jon Eby
ILLUSTRATOR
 Julius Ciss
PUBLISHER
 Quest Magazine

112 GRAPHIC EXCELLENCE

MERIT

ILUSTRATION

EDITORIAL PAGE

AWARDED TO
Julius Ciss
ART DIRECTOR
Jon Eby
ILLUSTRATOR
Julius Ciss
PUBLISHER
Quest Magazine

EDITORIAL PAGE

AWARDED TO
Julius Ciss
ART DIRECTOR
Rob Melbourne
ILLUSTRATOR
Julius Ciss
PUBLISHER
Today Magazine

MERIT
ILLUSTRATION

EDITORIAL PAGE

AWARDED TO
Doug Martin
ART DIRECTOR
Lindsay Beaudry
ILLUSTRATOR
Doug Martin
PUBLISHER
Key Publishers
CLIENT
Toronto Life Magazine

EDITORIAL PAGE

AWARDED TO
J. Rafal Olbinski
ART DIRECTOR / DESIGNER
Mitch Schostak
ILLUSTRATOR
J. Rafal Olbinski
PUBLISHER
Business Week

114 GRAPHIC EXCELLENCE

MERIT

ILLUSTRATION

EDITORIAL PAGE

AWARDED TO
James Tughan
ART DIRECTOR
Jackie Young
ILLUSTRATOR
James Tughan
PUBLISHER
Financial Post Magazine

EDITORIAL PAGE

AWARDED TO
Doug Martin
ART DIRECTOR / DESIGNER
George Haroutiun
ILLUSTRATOR
Doug Martin
PUBLISHER
Comac
CLIENT
Homemakers Magazine

MERIT

ILLUSTRATION

EDITORIAL PAGES

AWARDED TO
 Normand Cousineau
CREATIVE DIRECTOR
 Normand Cousineau
ART DIRECTOR / DESIGNER
 Gianni Caccia
ILLUSTRATOR
 Normand Cousineau
PRINTER
 Payette et Simms
CLIENT
 Les Éditions Vice Versa

EDITORIAL PAGES

AWARDED TO
 Stéphan Daigle
CREATIVE DIRECTOR
 Stéphan Daigle
ART DIRECTOR / DESIGNER
 Gianni Caccia
ILLUSTRATOR
 Stéphan Daigle
PRINTER
 Payette et Simms
CLIENT
 Les Éditions Vice Versa

MERIT

ILLUSTRATION

ADVERTISING POSTER
AWARDED TO
  Glenbow Museum
DESIGNER / ILLUSTRATOR
  Dennis Budgen
PRINTER
  Agency Press
COLOUR SEPARATOR
  2N Graphics
CLIENT
  Glenbow Museum, Calgary

EDITORIAL PAGE
AWARDED TO
  Ken Dallison
ART DIRECTOR
  Harvey Grut
ILLUSTRATOR
  Ken Dallison
CLIENT
  Sports Illustrated

MERIT
ILLUSTRATION

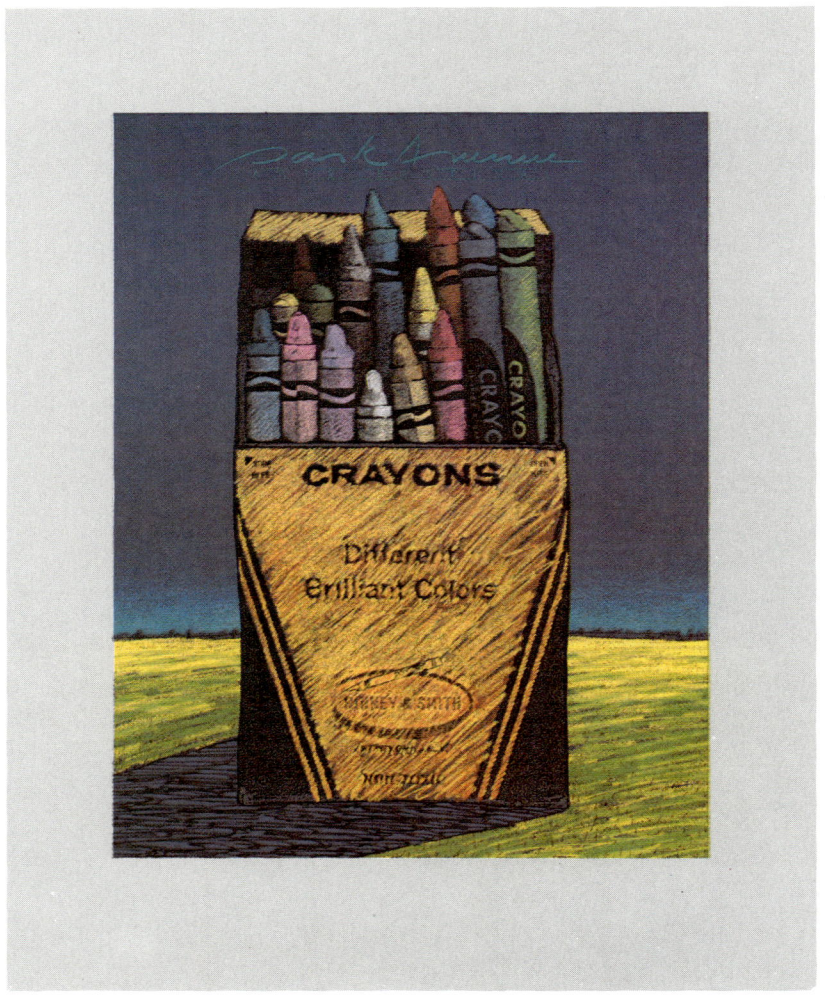

ADVERTISING POSTER
AWARDED TO
  Bob Conge
ART DIRECTOR / ILLUSTRATOR
  Bob Conge
PRODUCTION STUDIO
  Conge Design
CLIENT
  Park Avenue Merchants Assn.

GREETING CARD
AWARDED TO
  Bill Davis
CREATIVE DIRECTOR
  Glen Iwasaki
DESIGNER / ILLUSTRATOR
  Bill Davis
CLIENT
  NFL Properties

MERIT

ILLUSTRATION

POSTER
AWARDED TO
 J. Rafal Olbinski
ART DIRECTOR / DESIGNER
 J. Rafal Olbinski
ILLUSTRATOR
 J. Rafal Olbinski
PUBLISHER
 Papermania Studio
CLIENT
 Soshin Society

CALENDAR
AWARDED TO
 Tadami Yamada
ART DIRECTOR
 Mogens Sørensen
ILLUSTRATOR
 Tadami Yamada
PUBLISHER
 ScanDutch
CLIENT
 Thomas Bergsøe AS / JCA, Tokyo

MERIT
ILLUSTRATION

FRAMING PRINT

AWARDED TO
  Klaas Verboom
CREATIVE DIRECTOR / ART DIRECTOR
  Klaas Verboom
DESIGNER / ILLUSTRATOR
  Klaas Verboom
PRINTER
  Graphic Realm
COLOUR SEPARATOR
  Artcraft Engravers

SELF PROMOTIONAL

AWARDED TO
  John Fraser
ILLUSTRATOR
  John Fraser

MERIT

ILLUSTRATION

SELF PROMOTIONAL
AWARDED TO
Edith Simon
ILLUSTRATOR
Edith Simon

ILLUSTRATION 121

MERIT
ILLUSTRATION

MAGAZINE COVER

AWARDED TO
Industrial Management
ILLUSTRATOR
Simon Ng
CLIENT
Clifford Elliot Limited

SELF PROMOTIONAL

AWARDED TO
Mark Heine
ILLUSTRATOR
Mark Heine

MERIT

ILLUSTRATION

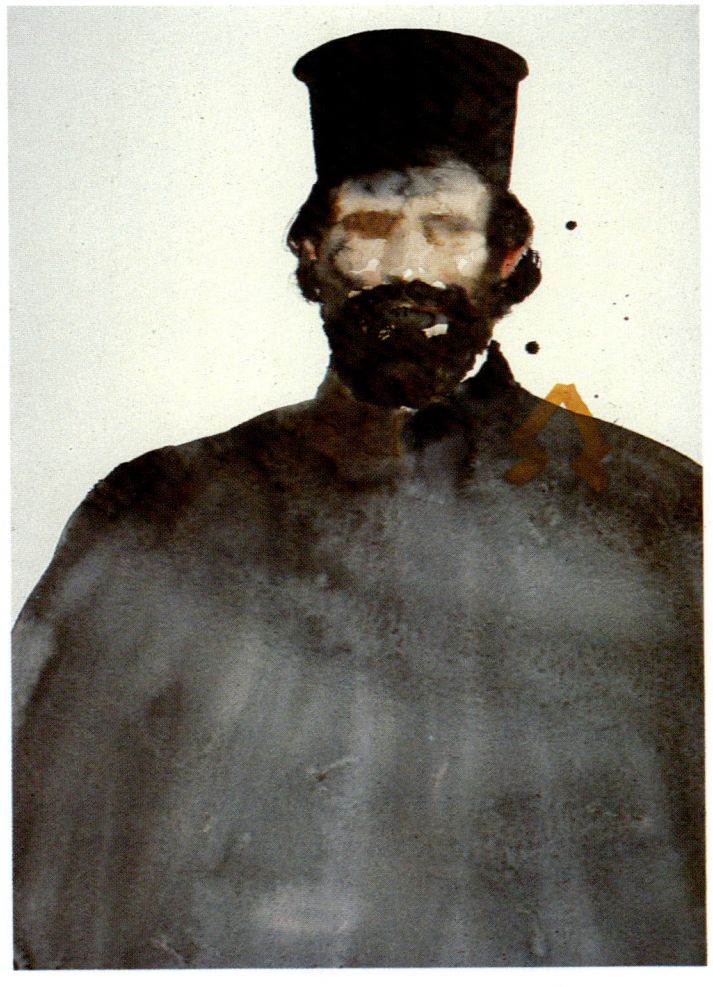

SELF PROMOTIONAL - SERIES

AWARDED TO
 Tom McNeely
ILLUSTRATOR
 Tom McNeely

MERIT
ILLUSTRATION

SELF PROMOTIONAL

AWARDED TO
Linda Kooluris Dobbs
ILLUSTRATOR
Linda Kooluris Dobbs

SELF PROMOTIONAL

AWARDED TO
Jane Chafe-Moote
ILLUSTRATOR
Jane Chafe-Moote

MERIT

ILLUSTRATION

SELF PROMOTIONAL

AWARDED TO
 Linda Scharf
DESIGNER / ILLUSTRATOR
 Linda Scharf
PRINTER
 Touchmark

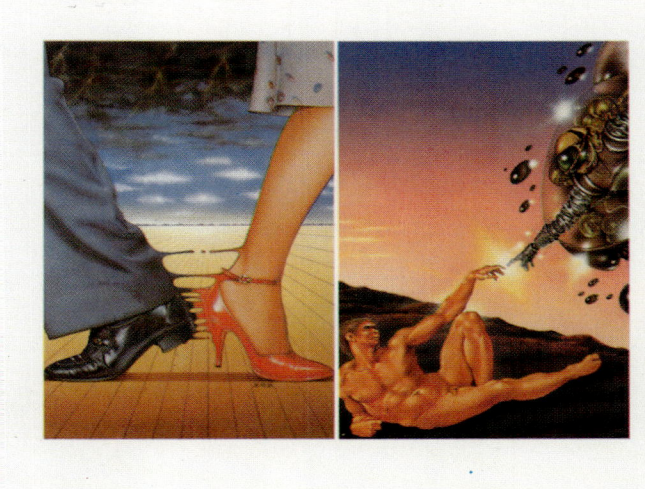

SELF PROMOTIONAL

AWARDED TO
 Fernando Medina
CREATIVE DIRECTOR / ART DIRECTOR
 Fernando Medina
DESIGNER
 Fernando Medina
ILLUSTRATOR
 Ramon Teja
CLIENT
 Ramon Teja Illustrator

CHAPTER 5
GRAPHIC EXCELLENCE

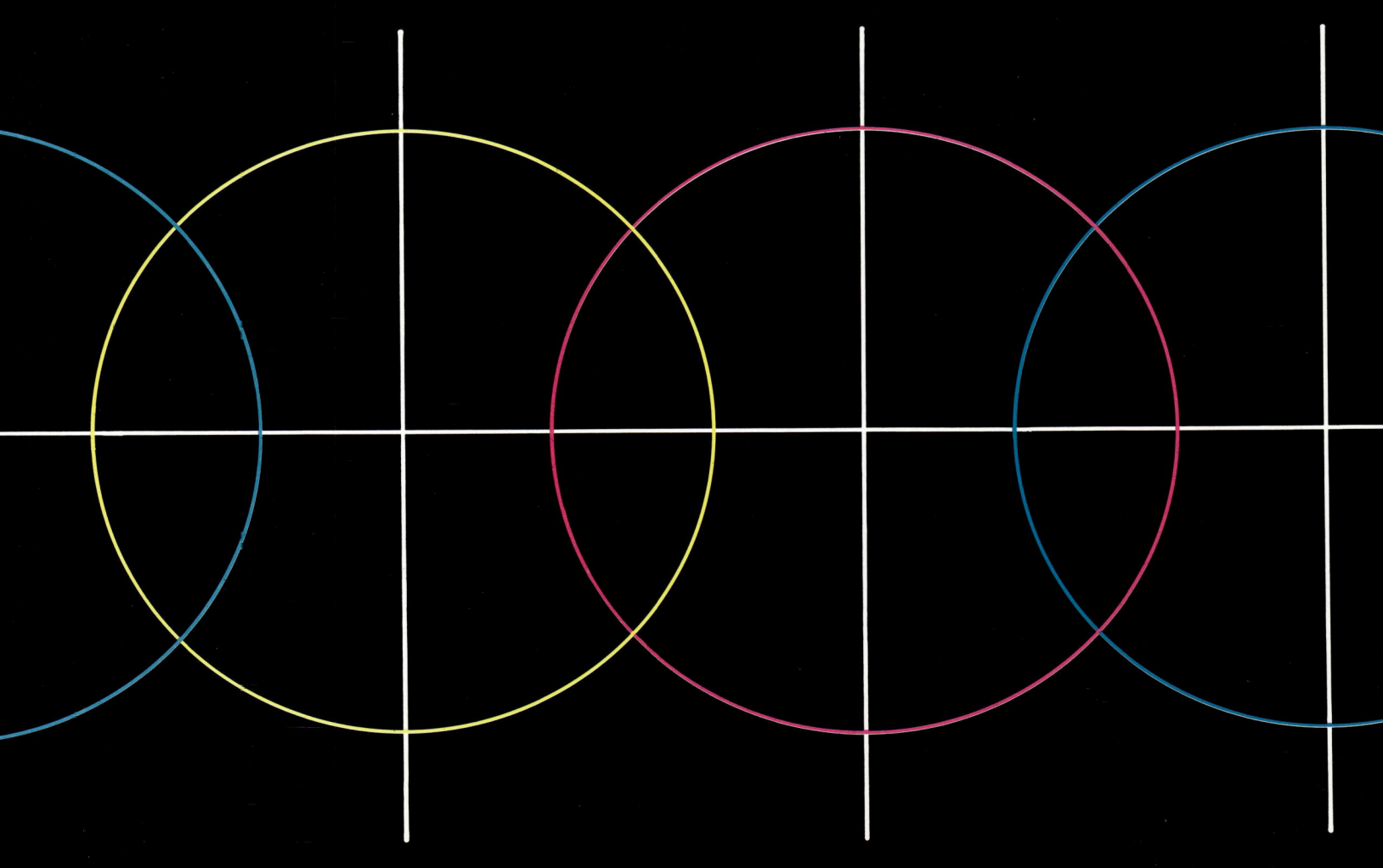

PRINTING

The technology of printing has changed and improved dramatically in recent years. Entries in this category were judged mainly on technical quality, and their merit is easily observed. Winners are from designations which include self-promotional, embossed/die cut, brochure, annual report, advertising poster, catalogue, consumer magazine, and stationery.

Several winners of silver and merit awards display technical excellence in various annual reports, and there are also several merit awards for brochures. Even when reproduced here, the quality of these pieces is obvious.

GOLD
PRINTING

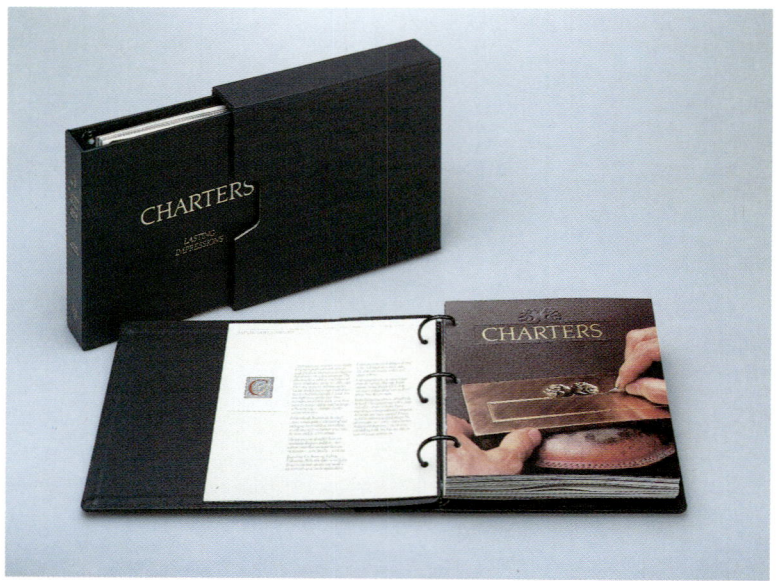

EMBOSSED / DIE CUT

AWARDED TO
 M.C. Charters & Co. Ltd.
ART DIRECTOR
 Robert Hyland
DESIGNERS
 Jon Vopni / Robert Hyland
PHOTOGRAPHER
 Peter Christopher
ILLUSTRATORS
 Jon Vopni / George Kay / Larry Bloss
 Frank Bonigut / Alf Ebsen
TYPOGRAPHER
 Type Studio Limited
WRITERS
 David Parry / James Hynes
PRINTER
 M.C. Charters & Co. Ltd.
 Herzig Somerville, Limited
COLOUR SEPARATOR
 Herzig Somerville Limited
DESIGN FIRM
 Robert Hyland Design & Associates
CLIENT
 M.C. Charters & Co. Ltd.

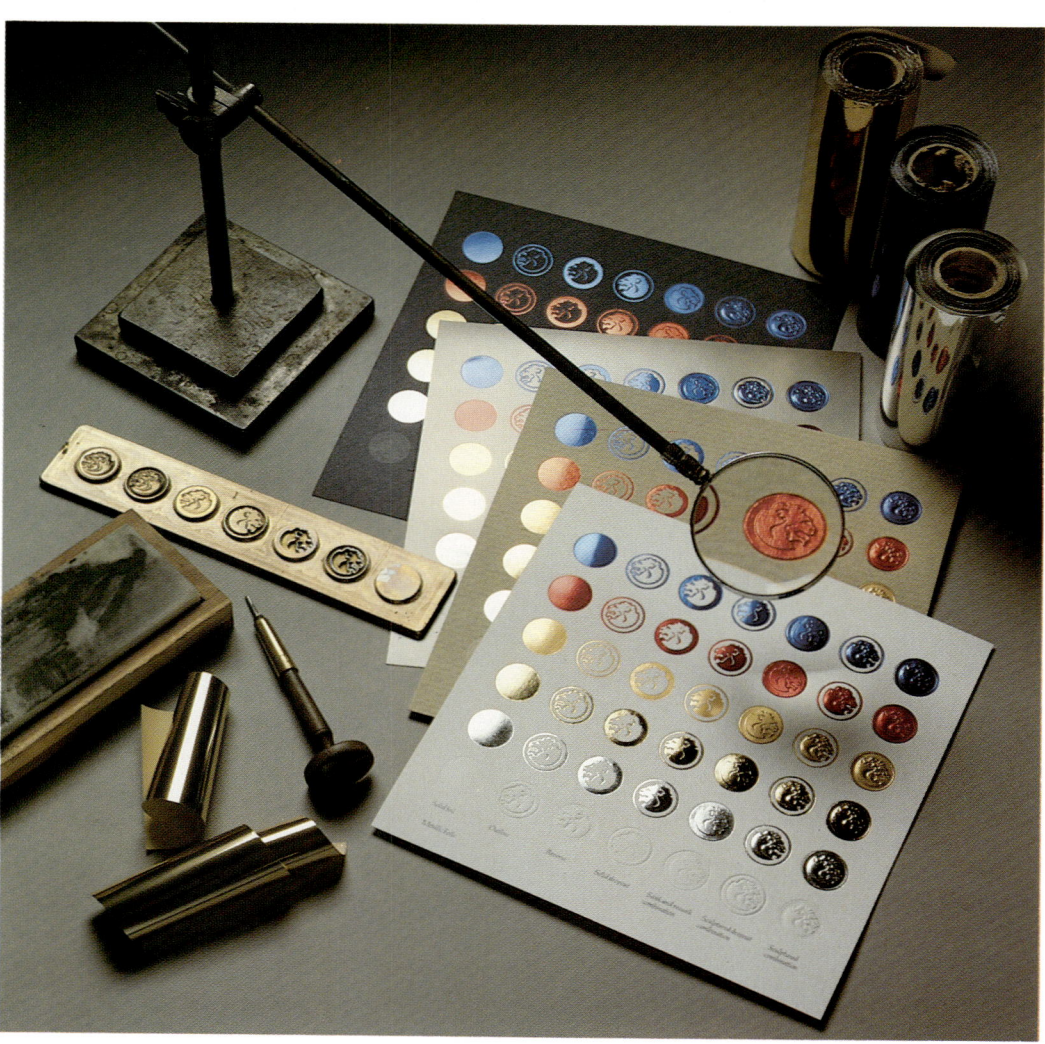

130 *GRAPHIC EXCELLENCE*

GOLD

PRINTING

SELF PROMOTIONAL

AWARDED TO
  Arthurs-Jones Lithographing Ltd.
DESIGNER
  Eskind Waddell
PHOTOGRAPHER
  Yuri Dojc
TYPOGRAPHER
  Cooper & Beatty, Ltd.
PRINTER
  Arthurs-Jones Lithographing Ltd.
COLOUR SEPARATOR
  Empress Litho Plate

April

SILVER
PRINTING

ANNUAL REPORT

AWARDED TO
  Arthurs-Jones Lithographing Ltd.
DESIGNER
  Taylor & Browning Design Associates
PRINTER
  Arthurs-Jones Lithographing Ltd.
COLOUR SEPARATOR
  Empress Litho Plate
CLIENT
  The Molson Companies

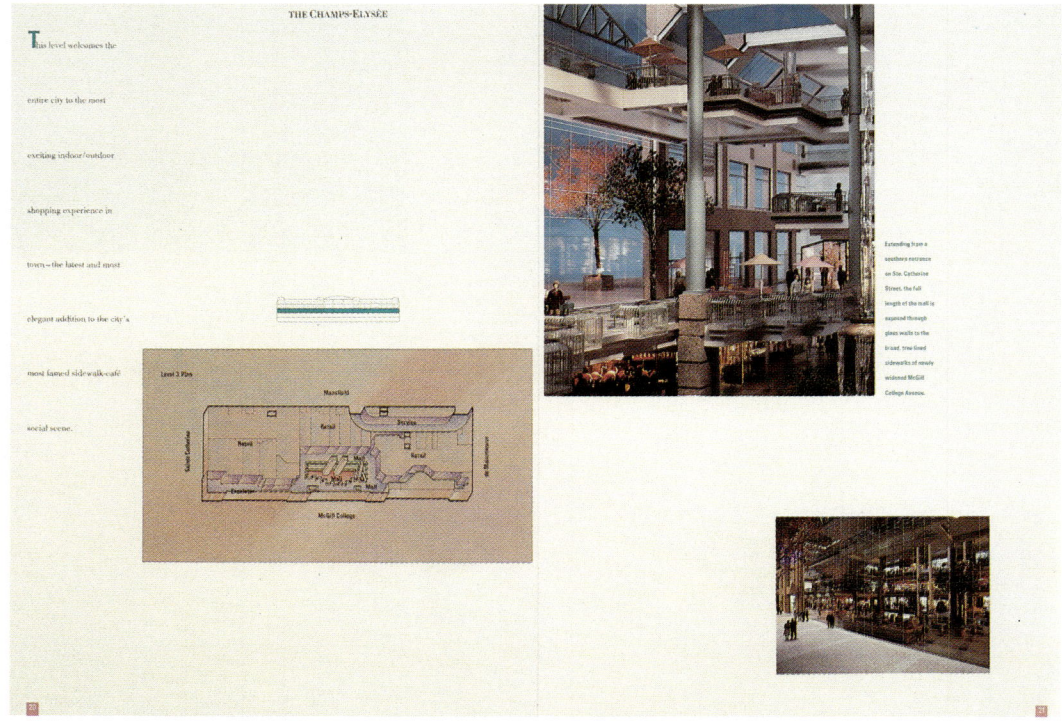

132 GRAPHIC EXCELLENCE

SILVER
PRINTING

BROCHURE
AWARDED TO
  Arthurs-Jones Lithographing Ltd.
DESIGNER
  Taylor & Browning Design Associates
PRINTER
  Arthurs-Jones Lithographing Ltd.
CLIENT
  Cadillac Fairview

SILVER
PRINTING

ANNUAL REPORT

AWARDED TO
  Arthurs-Jones Lithographing Ltd.
DESIGNER
  Eskind Waddell
PHOTOGRAPHER
  John Harquail
TYPOGRAPHER
  Cooper & Beatty, Ltd.
PRINTER
  Arthurs-Jones Lithographing Ltd.
COLOUR SEPARATOR
  Empress Litho Plate
CLIENT
  Toronto Dominion Bank

SILVER
PRINTING

ADVERTISING POSTERS - SERIES
AWARDED TO
  Arthurs-Jones Lithographing Ltd.
DESIGNER
  Del Terrelonge
TYPOGRAPHER
  Lind Graphics
PHOTOGRAPHER
  Ron Baxter-Smith
PRINTER
  Arthurs-Jones Lithographing Ltd.
COLOUR SEPARATOR
  Acme Graphics
CLIENT
  Lind Graphics

MERIT
PRINTING

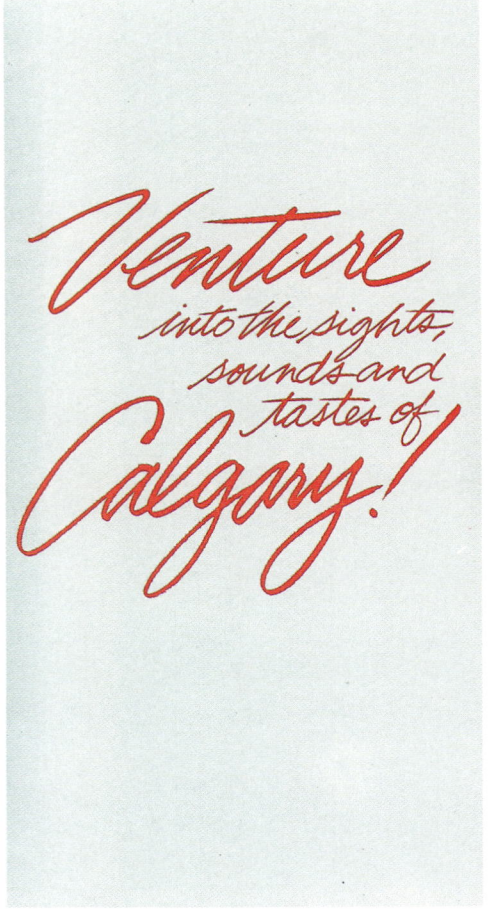

BROCHURE

AWARDED TO
  Paperworks Press Limited
PRINTER
  Paperworks Press Limited
COLOUR SEPARATOR
  United Graphic Services
ADVERTISING AGENCY
  Francis Williams & Johnson (Calgary)
CLIENT
  Calgary Convention Centre

MERIT
PRINTING

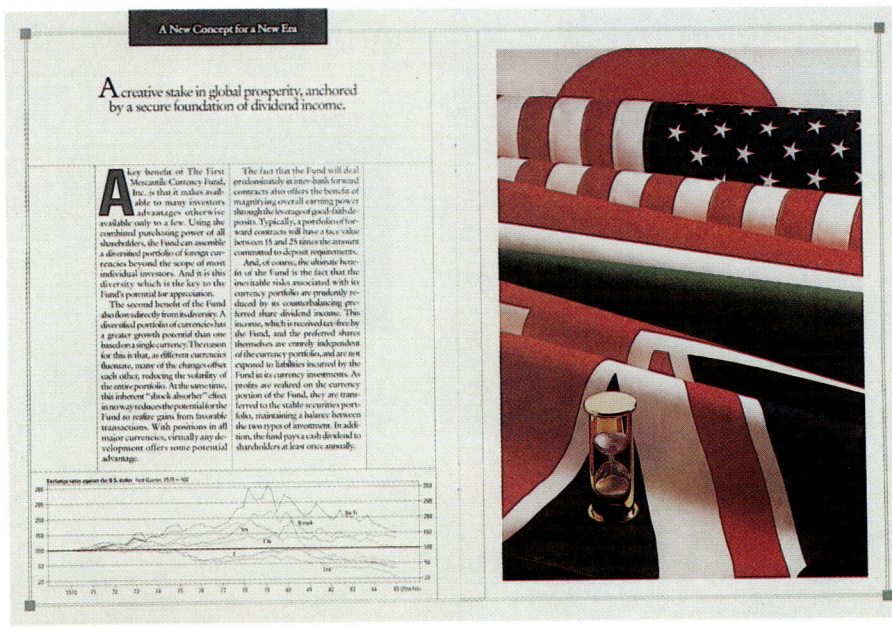

BROCHURE

AWARDED TO
  Provincial Graphics Inc.
PRINTER
  Provincial Graphics Inc.
ART DIRECTOR
  Paul Browning
DESIGNER
  Joe Drvaric
CLIENT
  First Mercantile Currency Fund, Inc.

BROCHURE

AWARDED TO
  Provincial Graphics Inc.
PRINTER
  Provincial Graphics Inc.
ART DIRECTOR
  Michael Malloy
DESIGNER
  Taylor & Browning Design Associates
CLIENT
  York Hannover Developments

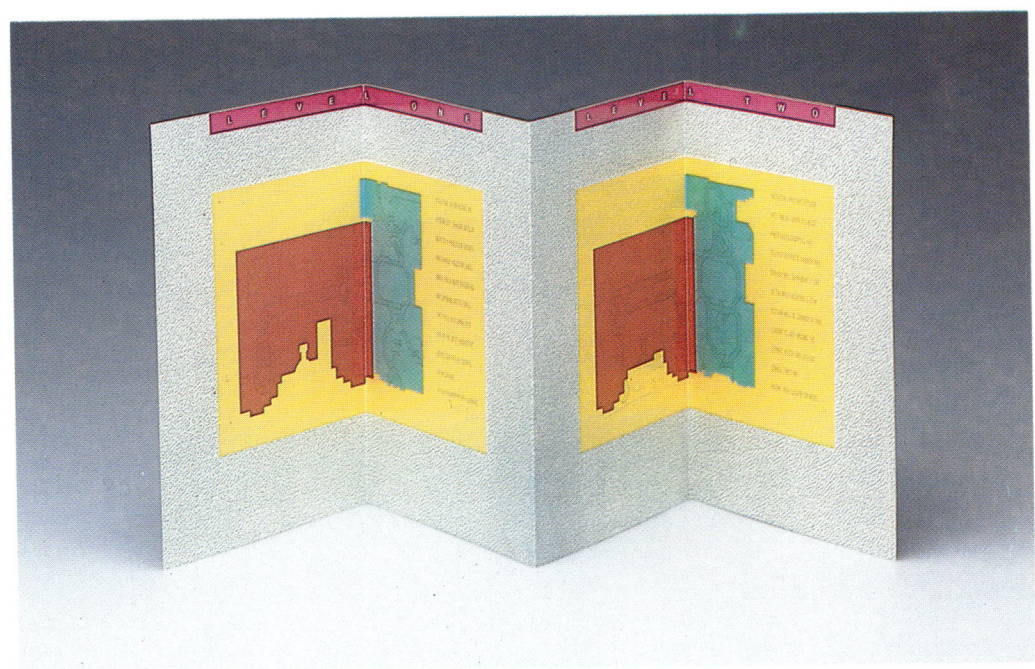

MERIT
PRINTING

BROCHURE

AWARDED TO
 Arthurs-Jones Lithographing Ltd.
DESIGNER
 Marck Campbell
 Adamson Industrial Design Inc.
PHOTOGRAPHERS
 Joe Duff - Format
 Hal Roth Photography Inc.
TYPOGRAPHER
 Typsettra Photocomp Ltd.
PRINTER
 Arthurs-Jones Lithographing Ltd.
CLIENT
 Adamson Industrial Design

BROCHURE

AWARDED TO
 Arthurs-Jones Lithographing Ltd.
DESIGNER
 Taylor & Browning Design Associates
PRINTER
 Arthurs-Jones Lithographing Ltd.
CLIENT
 Cadillac Fairview

138 GRAPHIC EXCELLENCE

MERIT
PRINTING

BROCHURE
AWARDED TO
  Arthurs-Jones Lithographing Ltd
PRINTER
  Arthurs-Jones Lithographing Ltd
CLIENT
  Canadian Kenworth Company

ANNUAL REPORT
AWARDED TO
  Arthurs-Jones Lithographing Ltd.
DESIGNER
  Taylor & Browning Design Associates
PHOTOGRAPHER
  Jim Allen
TYPOGRAPHER
  Cooper & Beatty, Ltd.
PRINTER
  Arthurs-Jones Lithographing Ltd.
COLOUR SEPARATOR
  Herzig Sommerville, Limited

PRINTING 139

MERIT
PRINTING

ANNUAL REPORT

AWARDED TO
Arthurs-Jones Lithographing Ltd.
DESIGNER
Eskind Waddell
PHOTOGRAPHERS
John Harquail / Dan Wiener / Yuri Dojc
TYPOGRAPHER
Cooper & Beatty, Ltd.
PRINTER
Arthurs-Jones Lithographing Ltd.
COLOUR SEPARATOR
Empress Litho Plate
CLIENT
Toronto Dominion Bank

ANNUAL REPORT

AWARDED TO
Arthurs-Jones Lithographing Ltd.
DESIGNER
Eskind Waddell
PHOTOGRAPHER
Daniel Wiener
TYPOGRAPHER
Cooper & Beatty, Ltd.
PRINTER
Arthurs-Jones Lithographing Ltd.
COLOUR SEPARATOR
Empress Litho Plate
CLIENT
Toronto Dominion Bank

MERIT
PRINTING

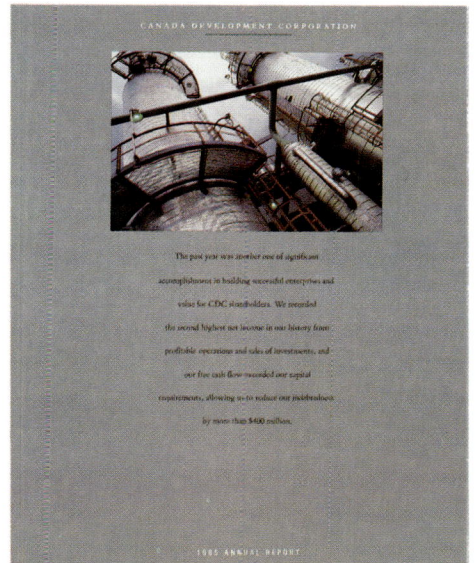
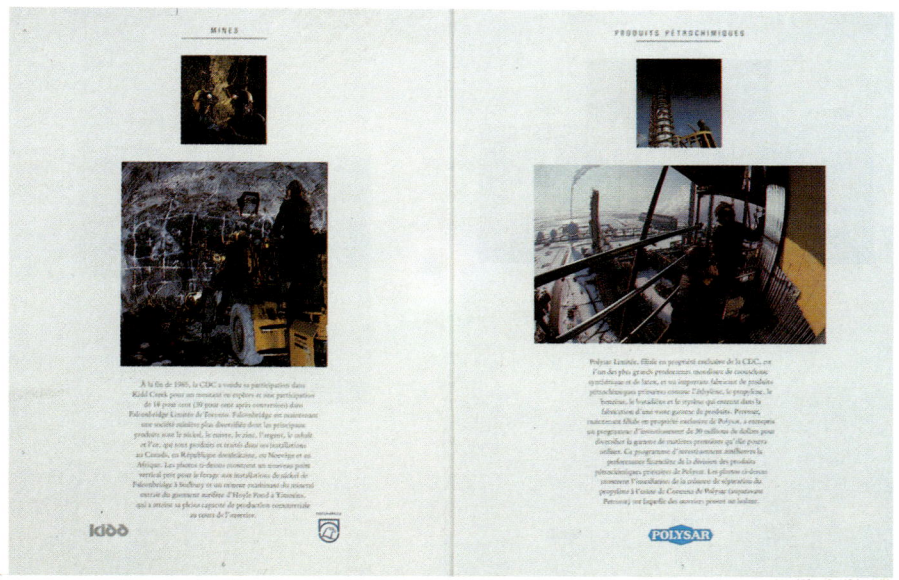

ANNUAL REPORT
AWARDED TO
  Arthurs-Jones Lithographing Ltd.
DESIGNER
  Eskind Waddell
TYPOGRAPHER
  Cooper & Beatty, Ltd.
PRINTER
  Arthurs-Jones Lithographing Ltd.
COLOUR SEPARATOR
  Empress Litho Plate
CLIENT
  Canada Development Corporation

ANNUAL REPORT
AWARDED TO
  Arthurs-Jones Lithographing Ltd.
DESIGNER
  Taylor & Browning Design Associates
PHOTOGRAPHER
  Robert Watson Photography
TYPOGRAPHER
  Cooper & Beatty, Ltd.
PRINTER
  Arthurs-Jones Lithographing Ltd.
CLIENT
  YMCA of Metropolitan Toronto

MERIT
PRINTING

ANNUAL REPORT

AWARDED TO
 Arthurs-Jones Lithographing Ltd.
DESIGNER
 Taylor & Browning Design Associates
PRINTER
 Arthurs-Jones Lithographing Ltd.
COLOUR SEPARATOR
 Empress Litho Plate
CLIENT
 Royal Bank

ANNUAL REPORT

AWARDED TO
 Maclean Hunter Printing
PRINTER
 Yorkville Press

MERIT
PRINTING

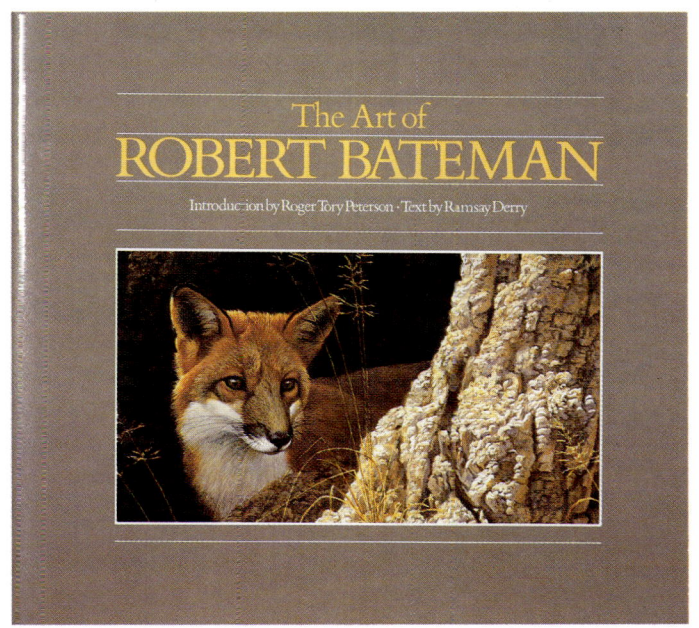

COMPLETE BOOK
AWARDED TO
  Arthurs-Jones Lithographing Ltd
ILLUSTRATOR
  Robert Bateman
PRINTER
  Arthurs-Jones Lithographing Ltd.
PUBLISHER
  Madison Press
COLOUR SEPARATOR
  Empress Litho

CONSUMER MAGAZINE
AWARDED TO
  Maclean Hunter Printing
ART DIRECTOR
  Marian Mustard
EDITOR
  Barbara Jean Neal
PRINTER
  Maclean Hunter Printing
PUBLISHER
  Bruce Lawrence Drane

PRINTING 143

MERIT
PRINTING

ADVERTISING POSTER

AWARDED TO
  Arthurs-Jones Lithographing Ltd.
DESIGNER
  Taylor & Browning Design Associates
PRINTER
  Arthurs-Jones Lithographing Ltd.
CLIENT
  Cadillac-Fairview

MERIT

PRINTING

BROCHURE
AWARDED TO
  Gaylord Corporate
DESIGNER
  Fisher Design Associates
PRINTER
  Gaylord Corporate
CLIENT
  Shell Canada

CATALOGUE
AWARDED TO PRINTER
  Arthurs-Jones Lithographing Ltd.
DESIGNER
  Gerry Mamone Design
CLIENT
  Holt Renfrew

PRINTING 145

MERIT
PRINTING

BROCHURE

AWARDED TO
 Arthurs-Jones Lithographing Ltd.
DESIGNER
 Taylor & Browning Design Associates
PHOTOGRAPHERS
 Jim Allen / Christopher Deer
PRINTER
 Arthurs-Jones Lithographing Ltd.

EMBOSSED - SPECIALTY ITEM

AWARDED TO
 M.C. Charters & Co. Ltd.
ART DIRECTOR
 Robert Hyland
DESIGNERS
 Alicia Tyson / Robert Hyland
PHOTOGRAPHERS
 Paul Orenstein / Peter Christopher
TYPOGRAPHERS
 Dave Thomason / Cooper & Beatty, Limited
PRINTERS
 M.C. Charters & Co. Ltd.
 Herzig Somerville, Limited
DESIGN FIRM
 Robert Hyland Design & Associates
CLIENT
 M.C. Charters & Co. Ltd.

MERIT
PRINTING

ART PRINTS FOR FRAMING

AWARDED TO
 Arthurs-Jones Lithographing Ltd.
DESIGNER
 Eskind Waddell
PHOTOGRAPHER
 Yuri Dojc
PRINTER
 Arthurs-Jones Lithographing Ltd.

ART PRINTS FOR FRAMING

AWARDED TO
 Arthurs-Jones Lithographing Ltd.
CREATIVE DIRECTOR / ART DIRECTOR
 Jim Donoahue
PRINTER
 Arthurs-Jones Lithographing Ltd.
CLIENT
 Jim Donoahue

PRINTING 147

MERIT
PRINTING

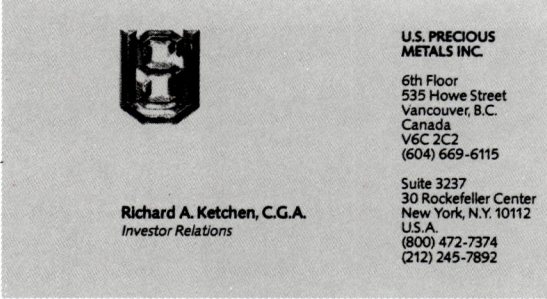

STATIONERY

AWARDED TO
  Samco Printers Ltd.
PRODUCTION STUDIO
  Samco Printers Ltd.
PRINTER
  Samco Printers Ltd.
CLIENT
  U.S. Precious Metals

STATIONERY

AWARDED TO
  Samco Printers Ltd.
PRODUCTION STUDIO
  Samco Printers Ltd.
PRINTER
  Samco Printers Ltd.
CLIENT
  Rocky Mountain Trout Farm

MERIT
PRINTING

STATIONERY

AWARDED TO
  Samco Printers Ltd.
PRODUCTION STUDIO
  Samco Printers Ltd.
PRINTER
  Samco Printers Ltd.
CLIENT
  Centurion Minerals

STATIONERY

AWARDED TO
  Adams Engraving Limited –
  S. Diane Denman
PRINTER / ENGRAVERS
  Adams Engraving Limited
CLIENT
  Celebrations

MERIT
PRINTING

SELF PROMOTIONAL
AWARDED TO
 Provincial Graphics Inc.
PRINTER
 Provincial Graphics Inc.
ILLUSTRATOR
 Thierry Thompson
CLIENT
 Provincial Graphics Inc.

MERIT
PRINTING

BROCHURE
AWARDED TO
  Provincial Graphics Inc.
ART DIRECTOR
  Scott Taylor
DESIGNER
  Joe Drvaric
PRINTER
  Provincial Graphics Inc.
  Holland & Neil - Silkscreening
CLIENT
  Sutter Hill Developments Limited

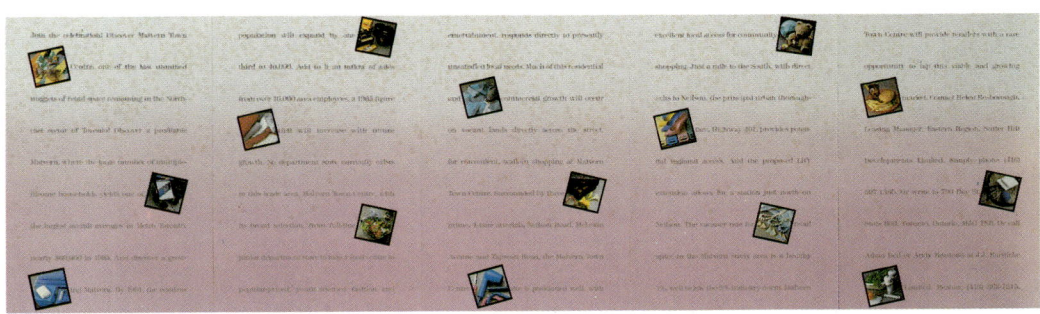

ADVERTISING POSTER
AWARDED TO
  Arthurs-Jones Lithographing Ltd.
DESIGNER
  Haughton Brazeau
PHOTOGRAPHER
  Ian Leith
PRINTER
  Arthurs-Jones Lithographing Ltd.
CLIENT
  Ian Leith & Associates

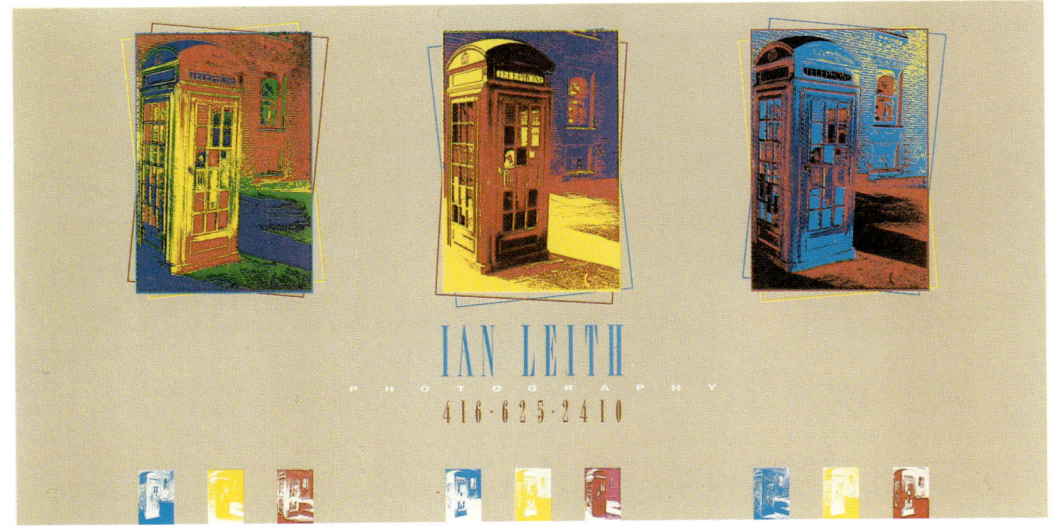

CHAPTER

6

GRAPHIC EXCELLENCE

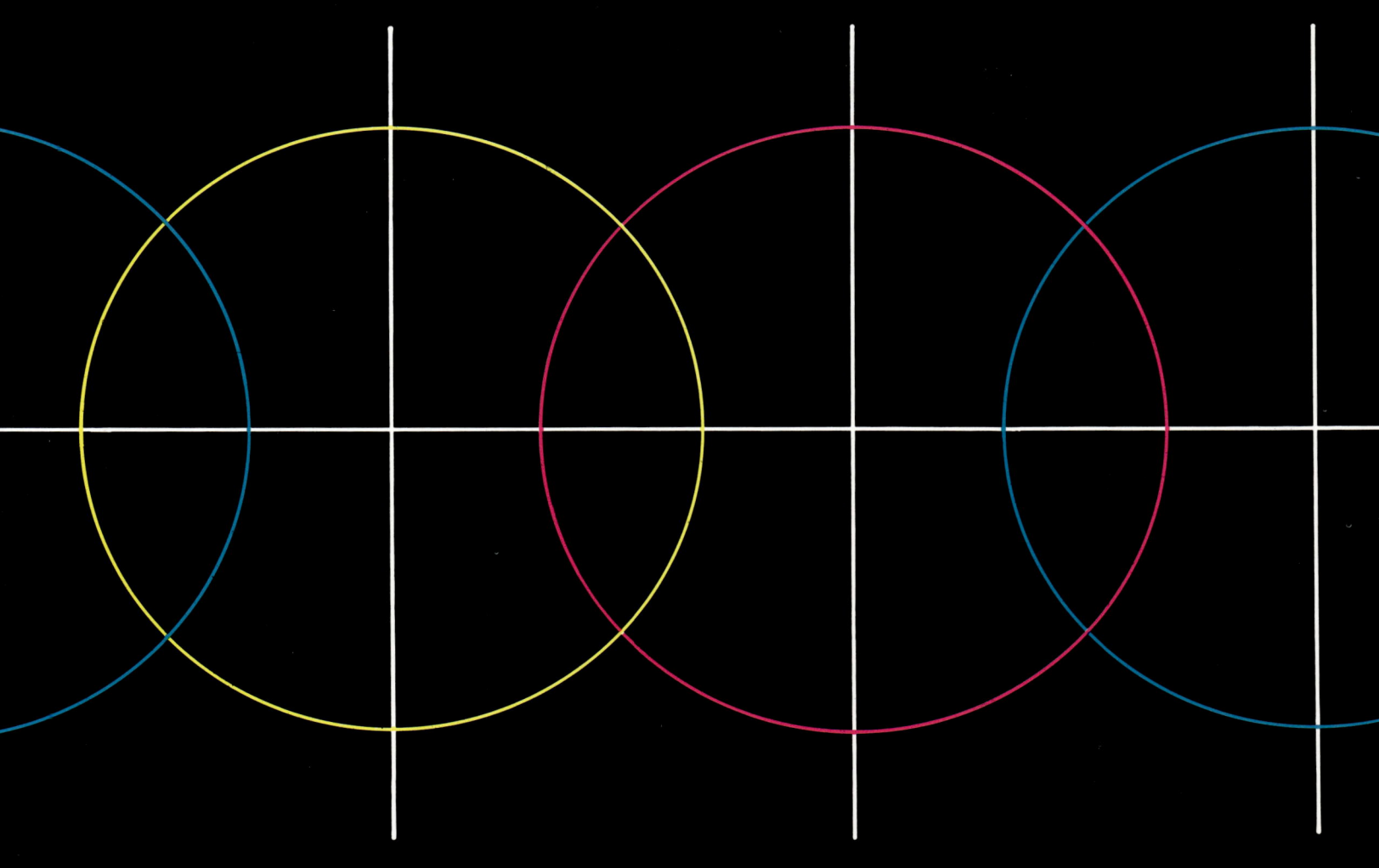

TYPOGRAPHY

This category covers various aspects of type used as design. Vividly illustrated are winning entries in designations including brochure, advertisement page, advertisement poster, handlettering, woodmark, and stationery.

The chapter displays a variety of uses and combinations of typefaces, from new and different color and type mixes to old typeface styles with a new look. Logotypes and stylized calligraphy are used artistically to create exciting design examples. Typography is presented here as the valuable communicator it has become.

MERIT

TYPOGRAPHY

BROCHURE

AWARDED TO
 Vopni & Parsons Design Limited
ART DIRECTORS / DESIGNERS
 Jon Vopni / Sandra Parsons
PHOTOGRAPHERS
 Philip Rostron
 Harthill Art Associates
 Stock
TYPOGRAPHER
 M & H Typography
PRINTER / COLOUR SEPARATOR
 Herzig Somerville, Ltd.
DESIGN STUDIO
 Vopni & Parsons Design Limited
CLIENT
 Provincial Papers

MERIT

TYPOGRAPHY

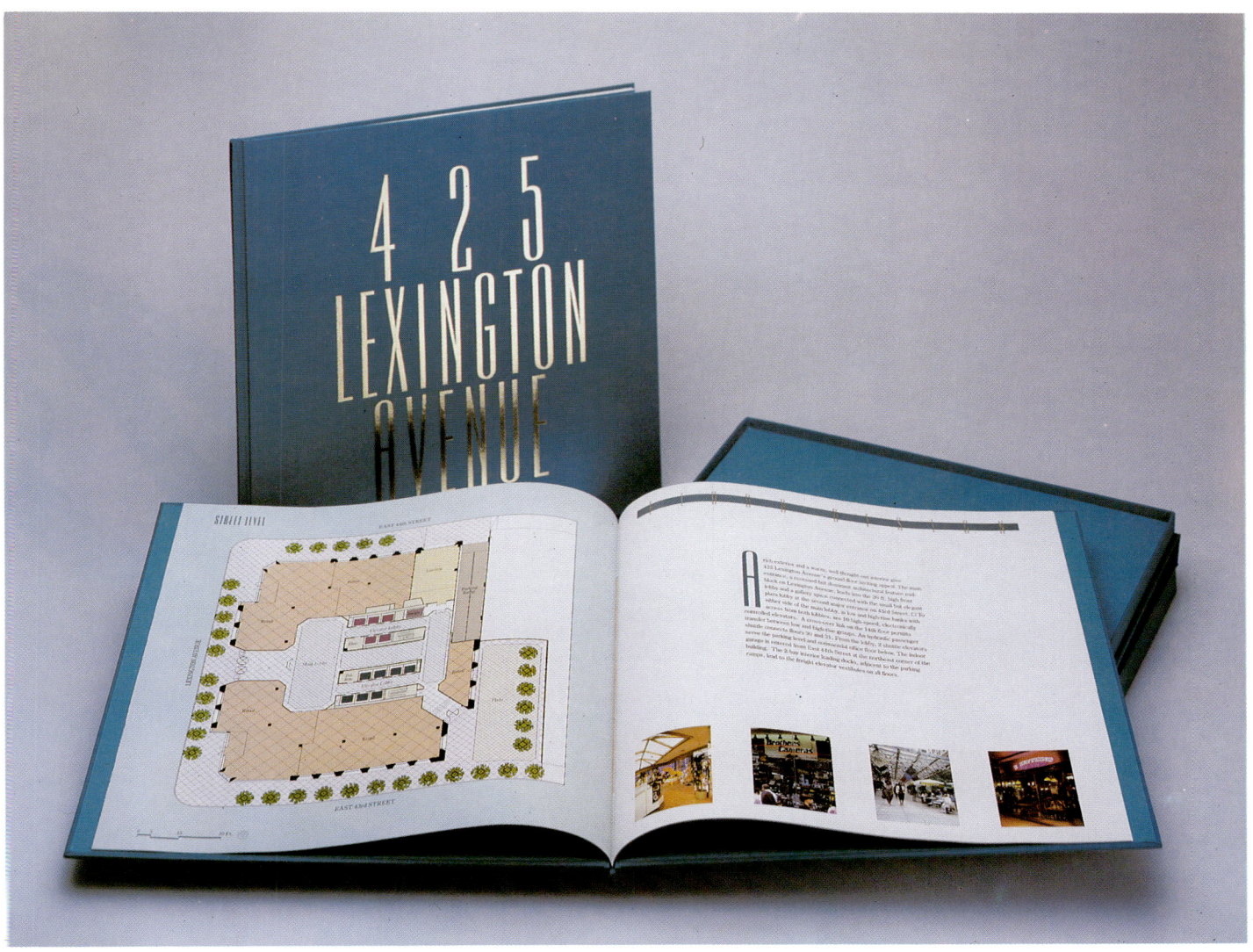

BROCHURE

AWARDED TO
  Jonas Tse Design Associates
ART DIRECTOR
  Simha Fordsham –
  Olympia & York Developments Ltd.
DESIGNER
  Jonas Tse
PHOTOGRAPHER
  Jeff Kellner
TYPOGRAPHER
  Dave Thomason
  Cooper & Beatty, Limited
WRITER
  Lorne Vineberg
CLIENT
  425 Lexington Ave. N.Y.

MERIT

TYPOGRAPHY

ADVERTISEMENT PAGE

AWARDED TO
   Scali, McCabe, Sloves (Canada) Ltd.
CREATIVE DIRECTOR
   Gary E. Prouk
ART DIRECTOR
   Andre Morkel
PHOTOGRAPHERS
   Ray Avery / Bruce Horn
ILLUSTRATOR
   Lou Normandeau - Retoucher
TYPOGRAPHER
   Typsettra Ltd.
WRITER
   Brian Quennell
ADVERTISING AGENCY
   Scali, McCabe, Sloves (Canada) Ltd.
CLIENT
   Apple Canada Inc.

MERIT

TYPOGRAPHY

As a teacher, I will not let this opportunity pass me by.
As a teacher, I will not let this opportunity pass me by.
As a teacher, I will not let this opportunity pass me by.
As a teacher, I will not let this opportunity pass me by.
As a teacher, I will not let this opportunity pass me by.
As a teacher, I will not let this opportunity pass me by.
As a teacher, I will not let this opportunity pass me by.
As a teacher, I will not let this opportunity pass me by.
As a teacher, I will not let this opportunity pass me by.
As a teacher, I will not let this opportunity pass me by.
As a teacher, I will not let this opportunity pass me by.
As a teacher, I will not let this opportunity pass me by.
As a teacher, I will not let this opportunity pass me by.
As a teacher, I will not let this opportunity pass me by.
As a teacher, I will not let this opportunity pass me by.
As a teacher, I will not let this opportunity pass me by.
As a teacher, I will not let this opportunity pass me by.
As a teacher, I will not let this opportunity pass me by.
As a teacher, I will not let this opportunity pass me by.
As a teacher, I will not let this opportunity pass me by.
As a teacher, I will not let this opportunity pass me by.
As a teacher, I will not let this opportunity pass me by.
As a teacher, I will not let this opportunity pass me by.
As a teacher, I will not let this opportunity pass me by.
As a teacher, I will not let this opportunity pass me by.
As a teacher, I will not let this opportunity pass me by.
As a teacher, I will not let this opportunity pass me by.
As a teacher, I will not let this opportunity pass me by.

Until December 31, 1984 every elementary, secondary
and university teacher in Canada will receive a substantial discount
on their choice of either an Apple® IIe or Macintosh™ computer.
See your participating authorized Apple dealer for details.
Opportunity only knocks once.

Apple and the Apple logo are registered trademarks of Apple Computer, Inc. Macintosh is a trademark licensed to Apple Computer, Inc.

Required reading for every Canadian teacher.

Until December 31, 1984 every elementary, secondary
and university teacher in Canada can receive a substantial discount
on an Apple® IIe or Macintosh™ computer.
The only requirement is that you bring a note from your principal
to your participating authorized Apple dealer.

Apple and the Apple logo are registered trademarks of Apple Computer, Inc. Macintosh is a trademark licensed to Apple Computer, Inc.

ADVERTISEMENT PAGE

AWARDED TO
 Scali, McCabe, Sloves (Canada) Ltd.
CREATIVE DIRECTOR
 Gary E. Prouk
ART DIRECTOR
 Tony Kerr
TYPOGRAPHER
 Typsettra Ltd.
WRITER
 Brian Quennell
PRODUCTION STUDIO
 Scali Art Services
ADVERTISING AGENCY
 Scali, McCabe, Sloves (Canada) Ltd.
CLIENT
 Apple Canada Inc.

MERIT

TYPOGRAPHY

ADVERTISING POSTER

AWARDED TO
　Carmen Jensen
ART DIRECTOR / DESIGNER
　Carmen Jensen
CLIENT
　National Action Committee on the Status of Women

MERIT

TYPOGRAPHY

SELF PROMOTIONAL

AWARDED TO
 Source Graphics Ltd.
CREATIVE DIRECTOR
 Herbert Graab
ART DIRECTOR
 Derek Browning
TYPOGRAPHER
 Keith Robinson
WRITER
 Herbert Graab / Derek Browning
PRODUCTION STUDIO
 Source Graphics Ltd.
PRODUCTION SUPERVISOR
 Herbert Graab
PRINTER
 Holland & Neil Ltd.

MERIT
TYPOGRAPHY

HAND LETTERING
AWARDED TO
  Robert Hyland Design & Associates
ART DIRECTORS
  Alicia Tyson / Robert Hyland
DESIGNER
  Alicia Tyson
TYPOGRAPHER
  Dave Thomason
PRINTER
  M.C. Charters & Co. Ltd.
DESIGN FIRM
  Robert Hyland Design and Associates
CLIENT
  M.C. Charters & Co. Ltd.
TYPESETTING
  Cooper & Beatty, Limited
PHOTOGRAPHERS
  Paul Orenstein / Peter Christopher

MERIT

TYPOGRAPHY

MAGAZINE MASTHEAD
AWARDED TO
 Vancouver Design Team Limited
ART DIRECTOR
 Don Dickson
DESIGNER
 William John Stewart
TYPOGRAPHER / PRODUCTION STUDIO
 Vancouver Design Team Limited
PRINTER
 Hemlock Printers Ltd.
PUBLISHER
 Journal of Commerce Publications
 Southam Communications Ltd.
COLOUR SEPARATOR
 Cleland Kent (Western) Ltd.
CLIENT
 Journal of Commerce Publications
 Southam Communications Ltd.

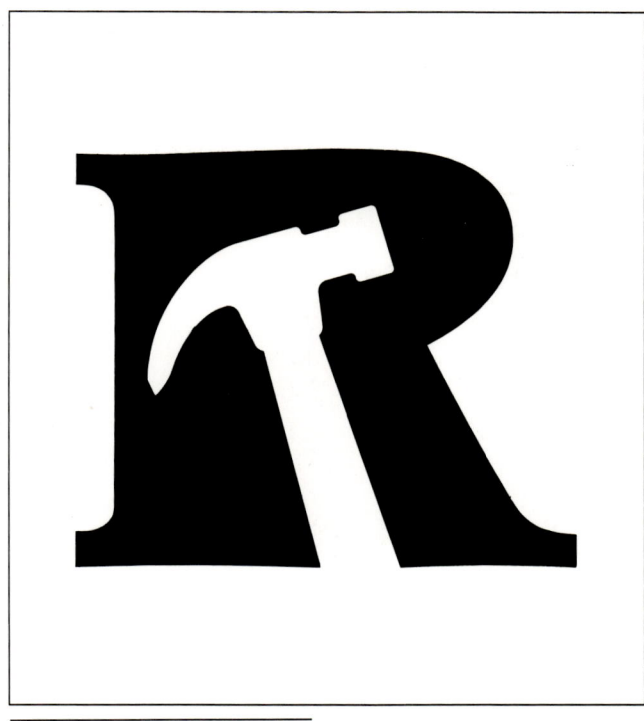

WORDMARK
AWARDED TO
 Peter Baker Design
CREATIVE DIRECTOR / ART DIRECTOR
 Peter Baker
DESIGNER
 Peter Baker
TYPOGRAPHER
 Headliners International
 Nick Shin – Gryphon
CLIENT
 Ross V. Roach Carpentry & Renovations

MERIT

TYPOGRAPHY

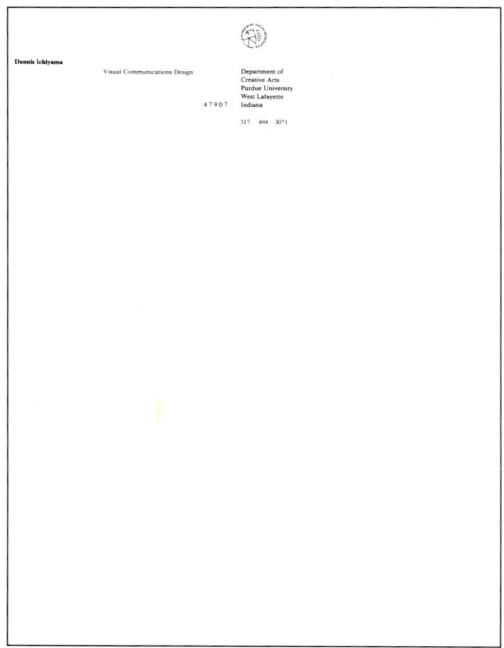

STATIONERY

AWARDED TO
 D. Ichiyama
CREATIVE / ART DIRECTOR / DESIGNER
 D. Ichiyama
TYPOGRAPHER
 Twin-City Typesetting
CLIENT
 Purdue University

STATIONERY

AWARDED TO
 Alpha Graphics Limited
DESIGNER
 Jim Donoahue
TYPOGRAPHER / CLIENT
 Alpha Graphics Limited

SELF PROMOTIONAL

AWARDED TO
 Alpha Graphics Limited
DESIGNER / WRITER
 Jim Donoahue
TYPOGRAPHER / CLIENT
 Alpha Graphics Limited

162 GRAPHIC EXCELLENCE

MERIT

TYPOGRAPHY

HAND LETTERING

AWARDED TO
  Hayhurst Communications Alberta Limited
CREATIVE DIRECTOR
  Trevor McConnell
CALLIGRAPHER
  Timothy Girvin
ADVERTISING AGENCY
  Hayhurst Communications Alberta Ltd.
CLIENT
  Alberta Human Rights Commission

CHAPTER 7
Graphic Excellence

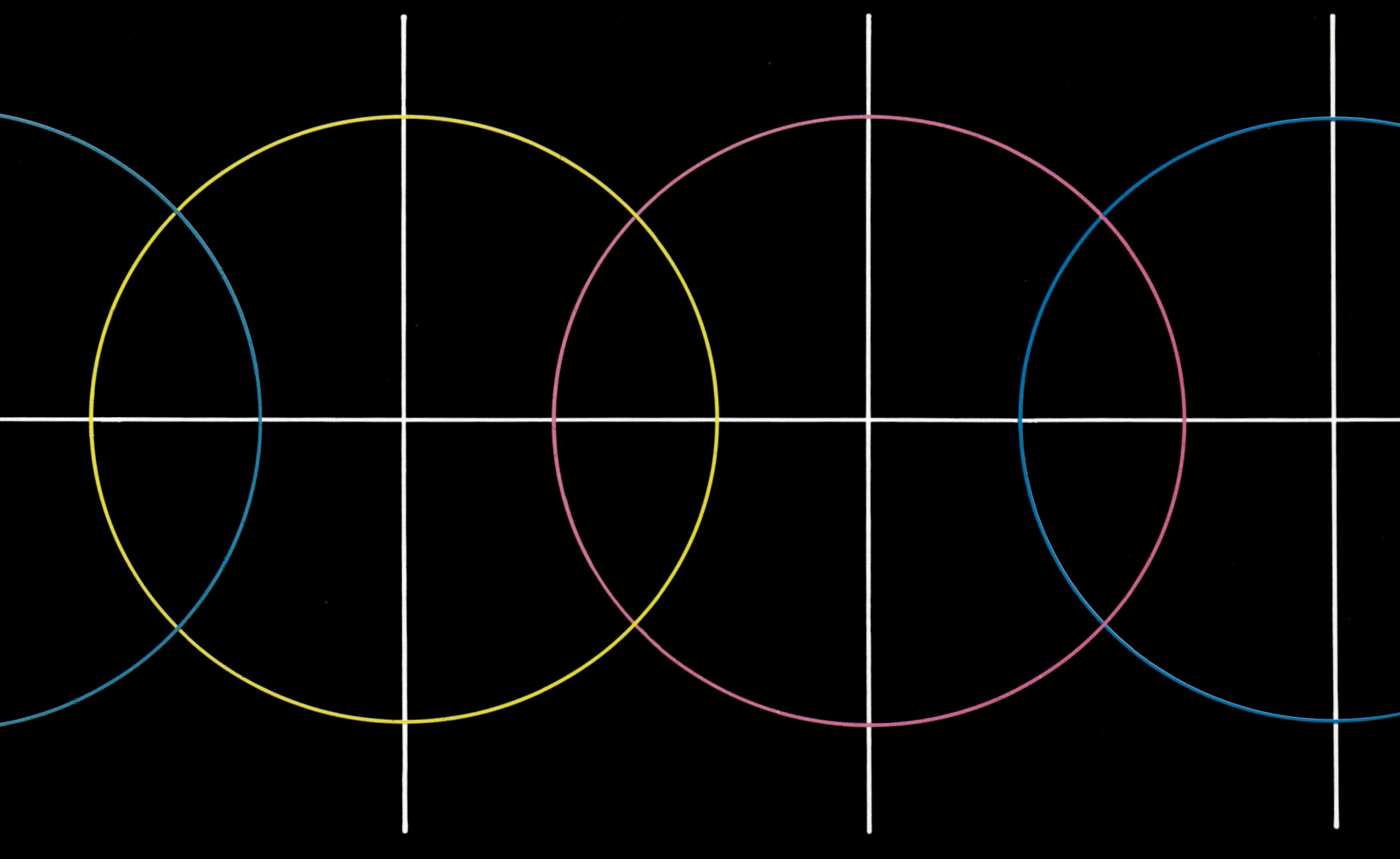

COPYWRITING

"Innovative approaches and appropriateness of the copy as it relates to the object of the communication" played an important role in judging this category. Winners were chosen in designations which include complete campaign, consumer advertisement, advertising brochure, outdoor advertising, and public service—series. The many award-winning consumer advertisements shown display attention-getting headlines which are fine examples of compelling, effective copywriting.

GOLD

COPYWRITING

As a teacher, I will not let this opportunity pass me by.
As a teacher, I will not let this opportunity pass me by.
As a teacher, I will not let this opportunity pass me by.
As a teacher, I will not let this opportunity pass me by.
As a teacher, I will not let this opportunity pass me by.
As a teacher, I will not let this opportunity pass me by.
As a teacher, I will not let this opportunity pass me by.
As a teacher, I will not let this opportunity pass me by.
As a teacher, I will not let this opportunity pass me by.
As a teacher, I will not let this opportunity pass me by.
As a teacher, I will not let this opportunity pass me by.
As a teacher, I will not let this opportunity pass me by.
As a teacher, I will not let this opportunity pass me by.
As a teacher, I will not let this opportunity pass me by.
As a teacher, I will not let this opportunity pass me by.
As a teacher, I will not let this opportunity pass me by.
As a teacher, I will not let this opportunity pass me by.
As a teacher, I will not let this opportunity pass me by.
As a teacher, I will not let this opportunity pass me by.
As a teacher, I will not let this opportunity pass me by.
As a teacher, I will not let this opportunity pass me by.
As a teacher, I will not let this opportunity pass me by.
As a teacher, I will not let this opportunity pass me by.
As a teacher, I will not let this opportunity pass me by.
As a teacher, I will not let this opportunity pass me by.
As a teacher, I will not let this opportunity pass me by.

Until December 31, 1984 every elementary, secondary
and university teacher in Canada will receive a substantial discount
on their choice of either an Apple® IIe or Macintosh™ computer.
See your participating authorized Apple dealer for details.
Opportunity only knocks once.

Required reading for every Canadian teacher.

Until December 31, 1984 every elementary, secondary
and university teacher in Canada can receive a substantial discount
on an Apple® IIe or Macintosh™ computer.
The only requirement is that you bring a note from your principal
to your participating authorized Apple dealer.

COMPLETE CAMPAIGN

AWARDED TO
  Scali, McCabe, Sloves (Canada) Ltd.
CREATIVE DIRECTOR
  Gary E. Prouk
ART DIRECTOR
  Tony Kerr
TYPOGRAPHER
  Typsettra Ltd.
WRITER
  Brian Quennell
PRODUCTION STUDIO
  Scali Art Services
ADVERTISING AGENCY
  Scali, McCabe, Sloves (Canada) Ltd.
CLIENT
  Apple Canada Inc.

COPYWRITING

CONSUMER ADVERTISEMENT
AWARDED TO
  Scali, McCabe, Sloves (Canada) Ltd.
CREATIVE DIRECTOR
  Gary E. Prouk
ART DIRECTOR
  Tony Kerr
PHOTOGRAPHER
  Yousef Karsh
TYPOGRAPHER
  Typsettra Ltd.
WRITER
  Brian Quennell
PRODUCTION STUDIO
  Scali Art Services
ADVERTISING AGENCY
  Scali, McCabe, Sloves (Canada) Ltd.
CLIENT
  Apple Canada Inc.

Macintosh and seven of its newest devotees. From left to right: Veronica Tennant, Charles Templeton, Peter C. Newman, A. Macintosh, Jack McClelland, Ben Wicks, Margaret Atwood, Harold Town. © 1985 Karsh.

Announcing the retirement of Canada's most famous typewriters.

Today, twenty-five of the finest imaginations in Canadian literature, art and broadcasting surrendered the traditional tools of their trade for Macintosh™ personal computers.

This historic event is only the beginning of a major commitment between the writers, editors and artists of McClelland & Stewart and the engineers, software wizards and computer evangelists of Apple Canada, Inc.

Which means that soon the entire McClelland & Stewart organization will be operating their business on the Macintosh Office network of hardware and software products.

In the meantime, Canada's finest minds are already busily creating words and pictures on the world's finest computer. And trying to find decorative uses for their typewriters.

Apple, the Apple logo and the Macintosh logo are registered trademarks of Apple Computer, Inc. Macintosh is a registered trademark licensed to Apple Computer, Inc.

SILVER

COPYWRITING

ADVERTISING BROCHURE
AWARDED TO
  Scali, McCabe, Sloves (Canada) Ltd.
CREATIVE DIRECTOR
  Gary E. Prouk
ART DIRECTOR
  Tony Kerr
PHOTOGRAPHER
  Olga Tracey
TYPOGRAPHER
  Typsettra Ltd.
WRITER
  Brian Quennell
PRODUCTION STUDIO
  Scali Art Services
ADVERTISING AGENCY
  Scali, McCabe, Sloves (Canada) Ltd.
CLIENT
  Apple Canada Inc.

SILVER

COPYWRITING

OUTDOOR ADVERTISING

AWARDED TO
 Scali, McCabe, Sloves (Canada) Ltd.
CREATIVE DIRECTOR
 Gary E. Prouk
ART DIRECTOR
 Tony Kerr
PHOTOGRAPHER
 Olga Tracey
TYPOGRAPHER
 Typsettra Ltd.
WRITER
 Brian Quennell
PRODUCTION STUDIO
 Scali Art Services
ADVERTISING AGENCY
 Scali, McCabe, Sloves (Canada) Ltd.
CLIENT
 Apple Canada Inc.

SILVER

COPYWRITING

We have enough sweaters to cut Toronto's heating bill 3%.

There are 302 stores in The Great Indoors.

We have a pair of oxfords for every scholar at U. of T.

There are 302 stores in The Great Indoors.

We have enough bathing suits for everyone in the Beaches.

There are 302 stores in The Great Indoors.

We have enough leather to supply everyone on Queen Street West.

There are 302 stores in The Great Indoors.

COMPLETE CAMPAIGN - SERIES
AWARDED TO
 Scali, McCabe, Sloves, (Canada) Ltd.
CREATIVE DIRECTOR
 Gary E. Prouk
ART DIRECTOR
 Karen Howe
TYPOGRAPHER
 Typsettra Ltd.
WRITER
 Peter Byrne
ADVERTISING AGENCY
 Scali, McCabe, Sloves (Canada) Ltd.
CLIENT
 The Eaton Centre

SILVER

COPYWRITING

We have more loafers than the Argos' defence.

There are 302 stores in The Great Indoors.

We sell more records than Anne Murray.

There are 302 stores in The Great Indoors.

We have enough pin-stripes to suit every banker on Bay Street.

There are 302 stores in The Great Indoors.

We could feed a sell-out crowd at the Gardens.

There are 302 stores in The Great Indoors.

SILVER

COPYWRITING

'Tis the season to be jolly...

At this very moment there are more than 500,000,000 children in 109 countries around the world living in misery. Lacking food, medicine, education – even hope. It's not necessary.

Give them a chance by buying UNICEF greeting cards designed by some of the world's leading artists. We're not begging you for a donation. We're asking that this season when you buy greeting cards, you look at ours. 20 beautiful, original designs that cost about $2.50 per set of ten cards. That's less than many commercial cards. And the same goes for our calendars, stationery and mini-note cards.

Call us at 366-3055 between 8:30 a.m. and 6:00 p.m. Monday thru Friday, or between 8:30 a.m. and 1:30 p.m. Saturday. Just ask for the UNICEF outlet nearest you. We're in more than 50 locations all over town.

Your phone call could save a child's life. Please help.

If you don't care, who will? Phone 366-3055 **Unicef Ontario**

Deck the halls with boughs of holly...

At this very moment there are more than 500,000,000 children in 109 countries around the world living in misery. Lacking food, medicine, education – even hope. It's not necessary.

Give them a chance by buying UNICEF greeting cards designed by some of the world's leading artists. We're not begging you for a donation. We're asking that this season when you buy greeting cards, you look at ours. 20 beautiful, original designs that cost about $2.50 per set of ten cards. That's less than many commercial cards. And the same goes for our calendars, stationery and mini-note cards.

Call us at 366-3055 between 8:30 a.m. and 6:00 p.m. Monday thru Friday, or between 8:30 a.m. and 1:30 p.m. Saturday. Just ask for the UNICEF outlet nearest you. We're in more than 50 locations all over town.

Your phone call could save a child's life. Please help.

If you don't care, who will? Phone 366-3055 **Unicef Ontario**

Don we now our gay apparel...

At this very moment there are more than 500,000,000 children in 109 countries around the world living in misery. Lacking food, medicine, education – even hope. It's not necessary.

Give them a chance by buying UNICEF greeting cards designed by some of the world's leading artists. We're not begging you for a donation. We're asking that this season when you buy greeting cards, you look at ours. 20 beautiful, original designs that cost about $2.50 per set of ten cards. That's less than many commercial cards. And the same goes for our calendars, stationery and mini-note cards.

Call us at 366-3055 between 8:30 a.m. and 6:00 p.m. Monday thru Friday, or between 8:30 a.m. and 1:30 p.m. Saturday. Just ask for the UNICEF outlet nearest you. We're in more than 50 locations all over town.

Your phone call could save a child's life. Please help.

If you don't care, who will? Phone 366-3055 **Unicef Ontario**

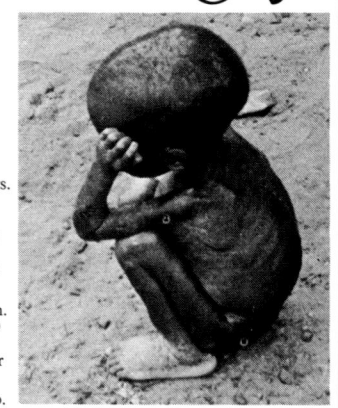

PUBLIC SERVICE - SERIES

AWARDED TO
  Wolf, Richards, Taylor
CREATIVE DIRECTOR
  Larry Wolf
ART DIRECTOR
  Colin MacLaren
WRITER
  Larry Wolf
ADVERTISING AGENCY
  Wolf, Richards, Taylor
CLIENT
  UNICEF

MERIT

COPYWRITING

CONSUMER ADVERTISEMENT
AWARDED TO
  Leon Berger / Mike Tott / Ron Caplan
  J. Walter Thompson - Montreal
CREATIVE DIRECTOR
  Leon Berger
ART DIRECTOR
  Mike Tott
WRITER
  Ron Caplan
ADVERTISING AGENCY
  J. Walter Thompson - Montreal
CLIENT
  Kraft Limited

MERIT

COPYWRITING

CONSUMER ADVERTISEMENT

AWARDED TO
  Scali, McCabe, Sloves (Canada) Ltd.
CREATIVE DIRECTOR
  Gary E. Prouk
ART DIRECTOR
  Andre Morkel
PHOTOGRAPHERS
  Ray Avery / Bruce Horn
RETOUCHER
  Lou Normandeau
TYPOGRAPHER
  Typsettra Ltd.
WRITER
  Brian Quennell
ADVERTISING AGENCY
  Scali, McCabe, Sloves (Canada) Ltd.
CLIENT
  Apple Canada Inc.

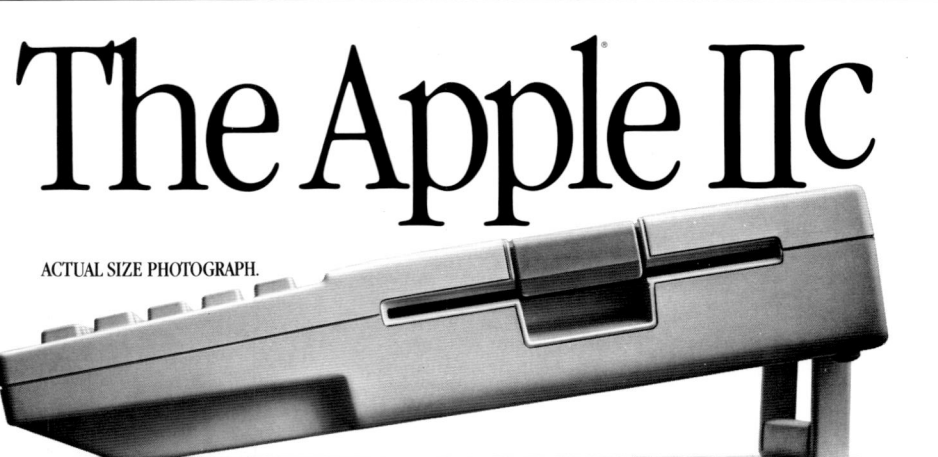

The Apple IIc

ACTUAL SIZE PHOTOGRAPH.

Under 8 lbs. Under $2,000.

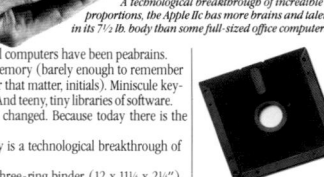

A technological breakthrough of incredible proportions, the Apple IIc has more brains and talent in its 7½ lb. body than some full-sized office computers.

Until now, most small computers have been peabrains. With 8 to 48K of memory (barely enough to remember their own names, or for that matter, initials). Miniscule keyboards. Puny displays. And teeny, tiny libraries of software.

Today all this has changed. Because today there is the Apple IIc.

The Apple IIc truly is a technological breakthrough of incredible proportions.

In the space of a three-ring binder (12 x 11¼ x 2¼"), it gives you the advanced technology of the world's most popular personal computer.

With 128K of RAM, it has twice the memory of computers that are twice its size. Its full-sized keyboard is every bit

Anyway you look at it, the Apple IIc offers more technology for your money. Like plug-in connectors that eliminate expensive expansion cards. Ever wonder why no one else shows you the back of their machine?

ACTUAL SIZE PHOTOGRAPH.

as comfortable as an IBM® typewriter (which is more than some have said for the personal computer of the same name). And its 80 column display makes the displays on other small computers resemble the bottom of an eye chart.

What's more, the Apple IIc comes complete with everything you need to begin computing right away. Including a built-in disk drive. An RF modulator that turns your TV into a monitor. A power supply pack. And four tutorial disks that teach you computing in a matter of hours. All in one box. All for under $2,000.

The brain behind the Apple IIc's 128K memory. A microprocessor with peripheral power to spare.

Once you've completed the tutorial, you can run your choice of more than 10,000 Apple II software programs. It's the largest library of software in the world. For business. Education. Home finance. And just for fun.

As your personal software library grows, so can your Apple IIc. Because it has the built-in electronics for virtually every peripheral imaginable. With simple plug-in connectors at the back. Adding peripherals has never been easier.

You never have to open up the machine. Or buy an expansion card. There are even little pictures above each connector that tell you exactly what plugs in where.

From Advanced Accounting to Zaxxon™ And everything in between. The Apple IIc lets you choose from the largest software library in the world.

If you're a real slave driver, you can drive your Apple IIc even harder and faster by plugging in a second disk drive.

If you're of the artistic bent, you can plug in a mouse and draw freehand illustrations in 16 colours.

If you have the killer instinct, you can add a joystick to shoot down dangerous aliens.

If you wish to communicate peacefully with other computers, you can add a modem.

To see your software program turned into hard copy, you can add a printer.

And regardless of what software program you're using, your Apple IIc will always give you a good point of view. Because in addition to your TV, you have a choice of displays.

There's the Apple IIc 9" Monitor with a high resolution green phosphor display and an adjustable stand for easy viewing. Or there's the Apple Colour Monitor with a high resolution RGB display that shows the IIc's true colours, much crisper than any TV. And soon to come, the IIc's own flat panel portable display. It snaps onto the top of the IIc and folds flat for travel. It's the first LCD display that shows as much as a regular monitor.

So as you can see, the Apple IIc keeps on growing more beautiful. Never before in recorded history has there been a computer this small, at this price, that could do this much. It really is worth a visit to your Apple dealer.

Apple IIc with monitor and mouse. Just one of the many possible configurations that let you adapt the Apple IIc to your specific needs.

Soon there'll be just two kinds of people. Those who use computers and those who use Apples.

MERIT

COPYWRITING

CONSUMER ADVERTISEMENT

AWARDED TO
  Scali, McCabe, Sloves (Canada) Ltd.
CREATIVE DIRECTOR
  Gary E. Prouk
ART DIRECTOR
  Michael Edwards
PHOTOGRAPHER
  Stanley Wong
TYPOGRAPHER
  Typsettra Ltd.
WRITER
  Peter Byrne
PRODUCTION STUDIO
  Scali Art Services
ADVERTISING AGENCY
  Scali, McCabe, Sloves (Canada) Ltd.
CLIENT
  Thomas J. Lipton, Limited

MERIT
COPYWRITING

CONSUMER ADVERTISEMENT

AWARDED TO
  Scali, McCabe, Sloves (Canada) Ltd.
CREATIVE DIRECTOR
  Gary E. Prouk
ART DIRECTOR
  Ken Boyd
PHOTOGRAPHER
  Stock (Sweden)
TYPOGRAPHER
  Hunter Brown
WRITER
  Terry Bell
PRODUCTION STUDIO
  Scali Art Services
COLOUR SEPARATOR
  Bomac Batten
ADVERTISING AGENCY
  Scali, McCabe, Sloves (Canada) Ltd.
CLIENT
  Volvo Canada Limited

MERIT

COPYWRITING

"How to count your chickens before they hatch."

By Richard Sharabura — Creative and Financial Strategist

A prominent financial strategist, Richard Sharabura is in the business of developing new businesses.

In nine months, the financial models Mr Sharabura created on the Apple® Macintosh™ have helped to double his firm's revenues.

Mr Sharabura is currently working on the financial models for five new private enterprises.

❝ The entire business of any business from our point of view is, 'What if?'
  'What if this happens?'
  'Or that happens?'
  'What if I do this?'
  'Or that?'

It's counting your chickens before they hatch.

If you're making a soufflé for fifty-two hungry auditors, you need to know how many eggs it's going to take.

You also need the resources to calculate how many eggs it'll take if ten or twelve decide to cancel out.

Accurate financial models for projecting, tracking and accounting are crucial to any business enterprise.

Whether it's a direct mail firm, a poultry farm or a neighborhood dry cleaner, you have to demonstrate to banks and investors that you have the analytical skills and business tools to make the correct decisions as circumstances change.

Apple's Macintosh is the only computer I know of that gives the small, private enterprise that degree of accounting power. In a machine that's usable by people whose primary business skill isn't a computer language.

That's why large financial corporations like Peat-Marwick are using Macs.

After all, when you think about it, the one difference between their books and yours, are the number of zeros at the end of the column.

As an example, one of the businesses we've developed is an extremely successful series of health reports sold through direct mail for a health care company in Charlottesville, Virginia.

Based on past experience, current production and postal rates and the dollar exchange, we determine a mailing's financial feasibility. Once the mailing is sent we track it against our projections.

At any given moment, on any particular mailing, we know whether we're making money and should continue to put our eggs in that basket or whether we're losing money and should invest elsewhere.

We've had several cases where our actual sales have dropped right on the dot of our projections. And happily, we've had several instances where they have exceeded our projections.

And that's just one of the businesses we're developing.

Anyone who dismisses the Macintosh as a serious number-cruncher hasn't taken a serious look.

Without the Mac, we simply couldn't be doing the quantity or quality of work we're doing now.

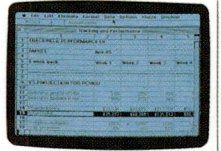

'Macintosh heightens, hones and enhances your analytical skills.'

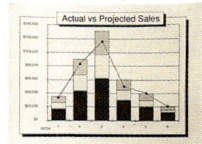

'The Macintosh can calculate the past, present and future. Across as many as 196 columns.'

Of course, you can still fail. But the guesswork is gone. Your data tells you what you need to know. In whatever form you find most understandable.

But more importantly, Macintosh opens your mind and lets you explore problems and opportunities in detail on levels that were previously unattainable.

If you locked me in a room with two thousand business people for an afternoon, I'm convinced they'd all walk out with Macs.

When you see what can be done first hand, you realize there are almost no limits to Macintosh's capabilities and what you can achieve.

And I'm not talking chicken feed. ❞

'For real communications power and impact, it's hard to compete with a Macintosh chart.'

As you've seen, the Macintosh has always delivered the power of sheer simplicity. Now, the Macintosh™ Plus delivers the simplicity of sheer power.

With a megabyte of internal memory. An 800K disk drive. Built-in networking capabilities. And a new expansion port that connects up to seven additional peripherals, including hard disks with tape back-up.

What's more, the Macintosh Plus is backed by the new full-year, cost-free AppleCare™ Warranty.

See your authorized Apple Dealer for specific coverage details.

Macintosh Plus and AppleCare. Because nobody cares for your business the way we do.

Apple and the Apple logo are registered trademarks of Apple Computer, Inc. Macintosh is a trademark of McIntosh Laboratory Inc. and is being used with its express permission. AppleCare is a service mark of Apple Computer, Inc.

CONSUMER ADVERTISEMENT

AWARDED TO
  Scali, McCabe, Sloves (Canada) Ltd.
CREATIVE DIRECTOR
  Gary E. Prouk
ART DIRECTOR
  Tony Kerr
PHOTOGRAPHER
  Olga Tracey
TYPOGRAPHER
  Typsettra Ltd.
WRITER
  Brian Quennell
PRODUCTION STUDIO
  Scali Art Services
ADVERTISING AGENCY
  Scali, McCabe, Sloves (Canada) Ltd.
CLIENT
  Apple Canada Inc.

MERIT

COPYWRITING

CONSUMER ADVERTISEMENT

AWARDED TO
  Scali, McCabe, Sloves (Canada) Ltd.
CREATIVE DIRECTOR
  Gary E. Prouk
ART DIRECTOR
  Andre Morkel
PHOTOGRAPHER
  Stanley Wong
RETOUCHER
  Lou Normandeau
TYPOGRAPHER
  Typsettra Ltd.
WRITER
  Brian Quennell
ADVERTISING AGENCY
  Scali, McCabe, Sloves (Canada) Ltd.
CLIENT
  Apple Canada Inc.

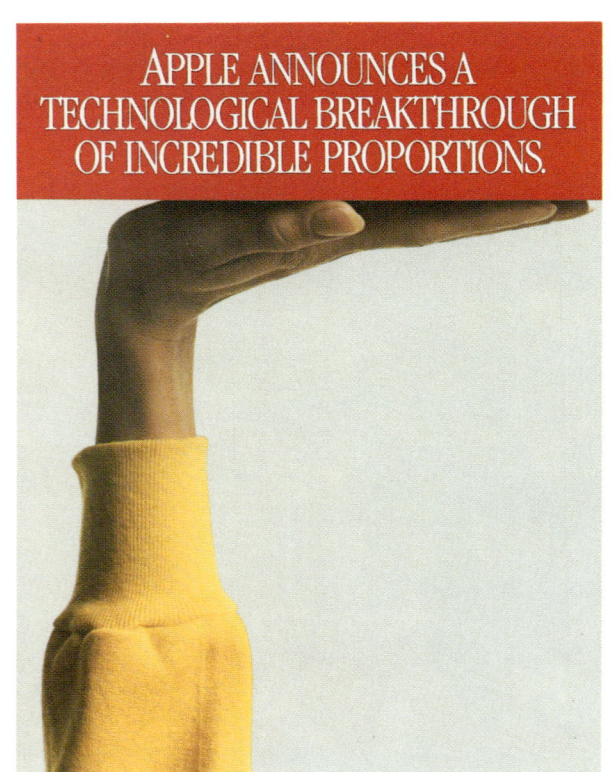

MERIT

COPYWRITING

The Apple II.
Because everybody operates at least one small business.

At first glance, these may not look like your average small businesses.

Until you begin to think of mortgage rates. Property taxes. Tuition fees. Home improvement costs. Car payments. And all the work that you don't get done at the office.

When you begin to add it up, an Apple® II personal computer suddenly begins to make a lot of sense.

An Apple II can help you express your thoughts with far greater speed, dexterity and elegance.

It can quickly juggle, toss and manipulate numbers. Not to mention storing vast amounts of information.

It can make home management simpler. And staying ahead at the office easier. Even when you're not there.

It can help your children achieve better grades. In fact, the Apple IIe is the leading educational computer in North America. Your children may be using one in school today.

What's more, an Apple II is the only personal computer that offers you the security of an eight year track record for reliability, expandability, and dependable dealer support.

The Apple II started the personal computer revolution in the seventies.

Today, it's leading the personal computer evolution. With a wide array of peripheral accessories. And the largest software base in the world.

There are more than 10,000 Apple II software programs in all. Including the best selling program in the world: AppleWorks.®

AppleWorks is an integrated software program that gives you word processing, spreadsheet and database capabilities all in one package.

It's incredibly swift, versatile and easy to use. And probably has all the computer applications you'll ever need.

There is one problem that may

The Apple IIc with optional Duodisk™
The Apple IIe with monitor and stand.

delay you from purchasing an Apple II.

And that's the tough decision of choosing between the Apple IIe or the more compact Apple IIc.

But if you visit an authorized Apple dealer, he, she or they will be more than happy to help you pick the one that's right for you.

After all, that's just good business. And we love good business.

Apply for an Apple Credit Card. Don't buy a computer without it.
Apple, the Apple logo and AppleWorks are registered trademarks of Apple Computer, Inc.

CONSUMER ADVERTISEMENT

AWARDED TO
  Scali, McCabe, Sloves (Canada) Ltd.
CREATIVE DIRECTOR
  Gary E. Prouk
ART DIRECTOR
  Tony Kerr
PHOTOGRAPHER
  Olga Tracey
TYPOGRAPHER
  Typsettra Ltd.
WRITER
  Brian Quennell
PRODUCTION STUDIO
  Scali Art Services
ADVERTISING AGENCY
  Scali, McCabe, Sloves (Canada) Ltd.
CLIENT
  Apple Canada Inc.

MERIT

COPYWRITING

COMPLETE CAMPAIGN

AWARDED TO
  Scali, McCabe, Sloves (Canada) Ltd.
CREATIVE DIRECTOR
  Gary E. Prouk
ART DIRECTORS
  Michael Fromowitz / Gray Abraham
ILLUSTRATORS
  Julius Ciss / Fausto Mourato
  Martin Hyde / G. Gauntlett
  Michelangelo Buonarroti
  Christine Bunn
WRITERS
  Gary E. Prouk / Hans Olaf Ein
PHOTOGRAPHER
  Nigel Dickson
RETOUCHER
  Bob Carmen
ADVERTISING AGENCY
  Scali, McCabe, Sloves (Canada) Ltd.
CLIENT
  Cadbury Schweppes Canada

MERIT

COPYWRITING

MERIT

COPYWRITING

PUBLIC SERVICE AD

AWARDED TO
Wolf, Richards, Taylor
CREATIVE DIRECTOR
Larry Wolf
ART DIRECTOR
Brian Brodber
WRITER
Larry Wolf
ADVERTISING AGENCY
Wolf, Richards, Taylor
CLIENT
NDP

Find out if you're a Conservative, Liberal or New Democrat.

For each of 15 issues listed below, check the statement (A, B or C) that comes closest to your own point of view. The answers are upside down at the bottom of the righthand column.

1. Oil Prices
- [A] Because we are 70% energy self-sufficient, we can keep our oil prices below world market levels to give Canadian business an advantage over foreign competition.
- [B] We need a blended price for oil based on a combination of foreign prices and replacement costs that may be higher or lower than world prices.
- [C] We need to raise oil prices $4 a barrel this year and $4.50 a barrel next year.

2. Energy Supply
- [A] We should build a pipeline to provide the Eastern provinces with surplus Western gas and reduce our dependence on foreign oil.
- [B] Although we have a lot more natural gas than we need, we probably should place some limits on what we sell just in case our calculations are wrong.
- [C] We have such a large surplus of natural gas that we can sell it to the United States for many years to come.

3. PetroCan
- [A] PetroCan's highly profitable retail operations should be expanded, so Canadians can buy gas from their own national oil company.
- [B] We need PetroCan to help us develop energy supplies, but we should leave the retail gasoline business to the multi-national oil companies.
- [C] The government should sell and give away 70% of PetroCan so it can be run as a private business.

4. Energy Development
- [A] PetroCan should save Canadians as much as $500,000,000 a year by taking over development of the Tar Sands.
- [B] We should guarantee the multi-national oil companies the profits they want to help us develop the Tar Sands.
- [C] The multi-national oil companies should develop the Tar Sands on their own without any government interference.

5. Cost of Living
- [A] Canadians should get up to a $358 tax credit related to indexed cost of living increases.
- [B] We may need wage and price controls again.
- [C] Canadians should get an energy tax credit of up to $80 per adult.

6. Interest Rates
- [A] Canada, like Switzerland or Germany, can set its own interest rates based on its own economic needs.
- [B] We must keep our interest rates 2 to 3% higher than the United States to prevent money from flowing out of the country.
- [C] When the United States raises its interest rates, Canada must follow to maintain economic stability.

7. Unemployment
- [A] Business tax incentives should be directly related to creating more Canadian jobs.
- [B] The government has done a lot over the past 10 years to create new jobs. Not much more can be done about unemployment.
- [C] If the government helps business earn more, job creation will take care of itself.

8. Inflation
- [A] The government should insure that consumers pay fair prices and roll back unfair price increases.
- [B] We may need wage and price controls again.
- [C] The best way to control inflation is to increase taxes and interest rates.

9. Canadian Resources
- [A] We can create jobs by processing Canadian resources into finished products here at home instead of exporting them to other countries.
- [B] We need to give foreign investors more tax and profit incentives to help us develop our Canadian resources.
- [C] The best way to maintain our standard of living is to increase the export of our natural resources.

10. Medicare
- [A] We need to stop doctors from double billing patients in excess of OHIP payments.
- [B] Doctors' fees are a subject for the medical profession and provincial governments to decide.
- [C] The government should not interfere in the doctor-patient relationship by setting fees.

11. Pensions
- [A] We need to increase old age pensions in proportion to the growth in wages and salaries.
- [B] We need an increase of $35 a month for single pensioners with no outside income.
- [C] We simply cannot afford any Federal pension increases right now.

12. Taxes
- [A] The loopholes that let multi-national companies get away with paying very little tax should be eliminated, so individuals can pay less taxes.
- [B] High income people need more tax shelter incentives to save and invest their money in Canada.
- [C] Business needs more substantial tax concessions and profit incentives to accelerate their investment in the economic development of Canada.

13. Small Business
- [A] We should make the chartered banks set aside a certain percentage of their loans for small businesses at reduced interest rates.
- [B] Small business really needs more government counselling and assistance in developing their export potential.
- [C] Banks should be given tax incentive to loan money to small businesses by not having to pay income tax on the loan profits.

14. Mortgages
- [A] Canadian families who earn less than $30,000 should get assistance in lowering their mortgage costs.
- [B] The government should not guarantee lower mortgage rates or provide any mortgage tax credit.
- [C] Everybody, no matter what their income, should pay the current bank mortgage rates. However, people with the highest mortgages should get up to a $1,500 tax credit for their interest payments.

15. Foreign Policy
- [A] We need to take co-ordinated trade and political action with other countries to show we will not tolerate Soviet aggression against neighboring states.
- [B] We should capitalize on our reputation as a peacekeeper to help alleviate international tensions and bring nations together.
- [C] We need to increase our defense budget by 17% and spend 4 billion dollars on American fighter planes.

Answers: The A answers are the New Democrat position, the B answers are the Liberal position, and the C answers are the Conservative position. This advertisement was paid for by the New Democrats.

MERIT

COPYWRITING

RECRUITMENT ADVERTISING
AWARDED TO
 Joanne Lehman
ART DIRECTOR
 Dick Amedeo
WRITER
 Joanne Lehman
ADVERTISING AGENCY
 Day Advertising Group, Inc.
CLIENT
 Bank of Montreal

MERIT

COPYWRITING

SELF PROMOTIONAL

AWARDED TO
  Caraway Kemp Winner Cline
CREATIVE DIRECTOR / ART DIRECTOR
  Clint Cline
DESIGNER
  Clint Cline
WRITER
  Nora Minor
ADVERTISING AGENCY
  Caraway Kemp Winner Cline
CLIENT
  Caraway Kemp Winner Cline

THIS IS BUSINESS-TO-BUSINESS COMMUNICATION
It's the color of your front door. The way your phones are answered. Your name. The way your people conduct themselves.
It's your business.
It's the way your product performs. It's an opinion. An impression. A memory. It's your advertising.
Good business-to-business communication can help you break through the clutter to grab a prospect's attention. Reinforce a customer's decision.
It's how you make a specific impression and impart vital information.
It's communicating what is special about your product, your service, your company and its people.
And it's letting the prospect in on the benefit. He wants holes, not drill bits.
Good business-to-business communication will generate prospects, and create recognition and awareness. It will spur action and, subsequently, more communication. Good communication keeps a customer satisfied, so that small problems are more likely to be forgiven. And the right communication thaws out the cold call by laying positive groundwork for the next step.
Business-to-business communication introduces facts and feelings that will favorably change the perception, the positioning of an offering in the reader's mind. It sets the stage to close the deal.
We're going to show you how it works. In fact, we've already begun.

THERE'S NOTHING USUAL ABOUT BUSINESS AS USUAL.
Although you may be just like your competition in a thousand other ways, there is at least one thing about your company that's different. Unique.
First, you need to understand precisely what it is that makes you different. Then, communicate that in a positive, memorable fashion. Is it image making? Image changing?
No.
It's only communication. Image starts right where you are. An advertising agency can't clarify your company's position in the mind of the consumer if it hasn't already jelled in the mind of your CEO. Your field engineer. Your order clerk.
And no amount of good advertising can sell a bad product. At least not twice.
An agency can only communicate what is.
But you must start with a clear statement of philosophy and a sharply defined image. Sit with your agency and come to terms – together – with what makes your product better. Unique. Understand why your people are special. Pinpoint – to the dime – who your prospects are, and what they want.
Then get going. You've got a story to tell.

O.K.
WE BOTH KNOW WHAT THE PRODUCT IS.
BUT WHAT ARE YOU SELLING?
Are you selling quarter-inch drill bits? Or quarter-inch holes? What's the end benefit to the user?
The compelling reason to make someone choose your product. Your service. Your unique selling proposition.
The tangible benefit is easy to define. What about intangible allure? Perfume promises romance. A computer offers efficiency.
And no one buys a Rolex just to tell the time.
On the other hand, many companies sell intangible products or services which must be made tangible in the minds of the consumer. The staid pinstripe your banker wears is tangible representation of the careful manner in which your money will be handled. The chocolate on your pillow in a five-star hotel is a visible reminder of the promise of attentiveness. And the carefully typed and bound proposal from your insurance broker is palpable evidence of interest, expertise and professionalism.
If your benefit – obvious as well as implied – is superior to your competition's, then you're certainly on the right track. But if it appears to be a dead heat, then you have only one choice.
Improve the communication of the benefit.
Now we're talking.

CREATIVE LEVERAGE: THINKING YOUR WAY THROUGH THE CLUTTER.
You can outthink your competition. Or you can outspend them.
If you choose to outthink them, then you better get some good thinkers on your team. Find creative people who take the time and initiative to acquaint themselves with your industry and its language. These are minimum requirements. There are more. That is, if you want your advertising to be extraordinary.
We all know what ordinary business-to-business ads look like. Ordinary. Since most are read in a business atmosphere while your reader is particularly receptive to information, they are often no more than informative. And often a lot less.
While dissemination of the facts is essential, that's where a lot of your competitors stop. They drop the ball. They misunderstand and neglect emotion, personality, positioning.
You can take that next step with the right creative team.
With the time-consuming, sweat-inducing search for the right words, the right visuals. The synthesis of facts and figures, meanings and feelings, information and inspiration into the right message. A message to break through the clutter of more than $3 billion worth of business ads run every year. A message fueled by a big idea, not just a big budget.
A fresh, compelling message to catch and keep the eye of your prospect.
And to catch and keep new business.

AFTER THE HONEYMOON.
NOW WHAT?
In their search for new and more business, many firms overlook their biggest resource: current business.
It must be remembered that, like a marriage, the sale is not the consummation of a process, but the beginning. For the buyer, the sale is the start of a relationship with the seller. And if you expect to keep his business, you'd better look at it the same way.
If you want your relationship to grow, talk to your client.
Talking is essential when things go wrong. And it's just as important when things go right. Ensure the client appreciates the good service he's getting. Keep him up to date on changes and news in the field. Ask his opinions.
Call. Visit. Write.
Your next sale, your next new customer, your next new product could depend on the communication you've fostered. Because if it's good communication, it goes both ways.
And it will make your marriage more rewarding than your courtship.

THIS IS HOW WE CLOSE.
Good business-to-business communication introduces new ideas. Reinforces them. Changes minds through presentation of fact and imagery. But more importantly, it generates inquiries.
So, the purpose of this piece is not so much to answer questions but to raise them.
To initiate discussion. Communication. Business-to-business communication.
Because the result of good business-to-business communication must be person-to-person communication. Although advertising can create awareness and desire, we all know it's a person who makes the sale.
Discuss this in your office. Then give us a call. There's a lot more we need to talk about.
Person-to-person.
Business-to-business.

MERIT

COPYWRITING

COMPLETE CAMPAIGN
AWARDED TO
  Scali, McCabe, Sloves (Canada) Ltd.
CREATIVE DIRECTOR
  Gary E. Prouk
ART DIRECTOR
  Andre Morkel
PHOTOGRAPHERS
  Richard Sharabura / Nigel Dickson
  Photo Researchers
WRITER
  Gary E. Prouk
ILLUSTRATORS
  Bill Payne / Bob Fortier
  Ted Michener / David Phillips
ADVERTISING AGENCY
  Scali, McCabe, Sloves (Canada) Ltd.
CLIENT
  Cadbury Schweppes Canada

THE ONLY PHOTO IN EXISTENCE ACTUALLY SHOWING HOW CADBURY GETS THE SOFT, CREAMY CARAMEL INSIDE THE CARAMILK BAR.

AFTER YEARS OF PUBLIC PRESSURE, CADBURY FINALLY EXPLAINS HOW WE GET THE SOFT, CREAMY CARAMEL INSIDE THE CARAMILK BAR. (IN CODE, OF COURSE. AFTER ALL, WE DON'T WANT EVERYBODY TO KNOW.)

FIVE GREAT PUZZLES BROUGHT TO YOU BY THE GREATEST PUZZLE OF ALL.

 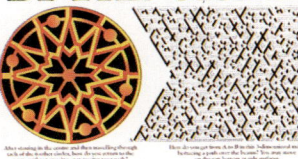  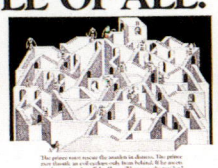 

SIX UNSOLVED MYSTERIES THAT SUGGEST EARTH WAS ONCE VISITED BY A SUPERIOR RACE.

   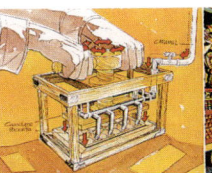 

FIVE METHODS WE DON'T USE TO GET THE SOFT, CREAMY CARAMEL INSIDE THE CARAMILK BAR.

ART DIRECTION
DIRECTORY

BERGER, LEON
Vice President/Creative Director
J. Walter Thompson
Company Limited
2060 Mountain Street
Montreal, Quebec, Canada
H3G 1Z7
Tel: (514) 844-2092

BOSADA, WAYNE
Greiner Harries MacLean
Advertising
4315 Village Centre Court
Mississauga, Ontario, Canada
L4Z 1S2
Tel: (416) 272-4972

BOUQUET, DAVE
J. Walter Thompson
Company Limited
2060 Mountain Street
Montreal, Quebec, Canada
H3G 1Z7
Tel: (514) 844-2092

BURNETT, NICK
Art Director
Maclean's Magazine
777 Bay St., 7th Floor
Toronto, Ontario, Canada
M5W 2B8
Tel: (416) 596-5350

BURT, JIM
Publiciti Watt Burt Inc.
1110, rue Sherbrooke Ouest
Montreal, Quebec, Canada
H3A 1G8
Tel: (514) 842-7876

CADE, PAUL
Doyle Dane Bernbach
Advertising Ltd.
77 Bloor Street West, Suite 1902
Toronto, Ontario, Canada
M5S 2Z8
Tel: (416) 925-8911

CAPLAN, RON
J. Walter Thompson
Company Limited
2060 Mountain Street
Montreal, Quebec, Canada
H3G 1Z7
Tel: (514) 844-2092

FURMAN GRAPHIC DESIGN
400 Slater, Suite 1902
Ottawa, Ontario, Canada
K1R 7S7
Tel: (613) 230-1384

GRANT TANDY LTD.
365 Bloor Street East
Toronto, Ontario, Canada
M4W 3L4
Tel: (416) 968-0201

HAYHURST
COMMUNICATIONS
(ALBERTA) LTD.
1040-7 Avenue S.W., #600
Calgary, Alberta, Canada
T2P 3G9
Tel: (403) 237-8200

HELMKEN, CHARLES
MICHAEL
Vice President
Council for Advancement and
Support of Education
11 Dupont Circle, Suite 400
Washington, DC 20036, U.S.A.
Tel: (202) 328-5911

ILES, TERRY
Art Director
Doyle Dane Bernbach
Advertising Ltd.
77 Bloor St. W.
Suite 1902
Toronto, Ontario, Canada
M5S 2Z8
Tel: (416) 925-8911

KAISER, URSULA
House & Home Magazine
20 Holly Street, #200
Toronto, Ontario, Canada
M4S 2E6
Tel: (416) 487-3621

KAZMER, ALLAN
Doyle Dane Bernbach
Advertising Ltd.
77 Bloor St. W.
Suite 1902
Toronto, Ontario, Canada
M5S 2Z8
Tel: (416) 925-8911

LAVOIE, PAUL
J. Walter Thompson
Company Limited
2060 Mountain Street
Montreal, Quebec, Canada
H3G 1Z7
Tel: (514) 844-2092

NICKLEN, BAMBI
Art Director
WEST, San Jose Mercury News
750 Ridder Park Drive
San Jose, CA 95190, U.S.A.
Tel: (408) 920-5795

PRITCHARD, JANE
J. Walter Thompson
Company Limited
160 Bloor Street East
Toronto, Ontario, Canada
M4W 3P7
Tel: (416) 920-9171

RAMSDEN, JIM
Art Director
BFS Advertising
208 Horseley Hill Drive
Scarborough, Ontario, Canada
M1B 1W6
Tel: (416) 291-1496

SCALI, McCABE, SLOVES
(CANADA) LTD.
2 St. Clair Avenue East
8th Floor
Toronto, Ontario, Canada
M4T 2T5
Tel: (416) 961-3817

TATE, VIV
Doyle Dane Bernbach
Advertising Ltd.
77 Bloor Street West
Suite 1902
Toronto, Ontario, Canada
M5S 2Z8
Tel: (416) 925-8911

TERRY O COMMUNICATIONS
INC.
195 Church Street
Toronto, Ontario, Canada
M5B 1Y7
Tel: (416) 864-0488

THURSBY, STEVE
Doyle Dane Bernbach
Advertising Ltd.
77 Bloor St. W.
Suite 1902
Toronto, Ontario, Canada
M5S 2Z8
Tel: (416) 925-8911

TOMALTY, TERRY
J. Walter Thompson
Company Limited
2060 Mountain Street
Montreal, Quebec, Canada
H3G 1Z7
Tel: (514) 844-2092

VOPNI & PARSONS
DESIGN LIMITED
518 Eglinton Ave. E.
Toronto, Ontario, Canada
M4P 1N6
Tel: (416) 483-6557

J. WALTER THOMPSON
COMPANY LIMITED
160 Bloor Street East
Toronto, Ontario, Canada
M4W 3P7
Tel: (416) 920-9171

WIESE, JERRY
Art Director
J. Walter Thompson
Company Limited
160 Bloor Street East
Toronto, Ontario, Canada
M4W 3P7
Tel: (416) 920-9171

GRAPHIC DESIGN
DIRECTORY

AMES, ANN
Ann Ames Design Associates Inc.
1110 Yonge Street
Toronto, Ontario, Canada
M4W 2L6
Tel: (416) 928-3282

BRAISE, THOMAS
President
Thomas Braise Photography
1824 El Verano Way
Belmont, California 94002, U.S.A.
Tel: (415) 591-4982

COLONNA, RALPH
President
Colonna, Farrell Design Associates
1335 Main Street
St. Helena, California 94574,
U.S.A.
Tel: (707) 963-2077

CONGE DESIGN
28 Harper Street
Rochester, New York 14607, U.S.A.
Tel: (716) 473-0291

DESIGNSOURCE
77 Mowat Avenue, Suite 304
Toronto, Ontario, Canada
M6K 3E3
Tel: (416) 537-7616

DIMSON, THEO
President
Theo Dimson Design Inc.
96 Avenue Road
Toronto, Ontario, Canada
M5R 2H3
Tel: (416) 923-2427

DUNJKO, CARMEN
Art Director
Carmen Dunkjo Associates Ltd.
66 Gerrard Street East, Suite 300
Toronto, Ontario, Canada
M5B 1G3
Tel: (416) 977-0767

EVANS, STEVEN
Steven Evans Photography Inc.
27 Davies Avenue
Toronto, Ontario, Canada
M4M 2A9
Tel: (416) 463-4493

GELLEN, ALEX
President
Alex Gellen Design
35 E. Seventh Street, Suite 704
Cincinnati, Ohio 45202, U.S.A.
Tel: (513) 651-1308

GOODWIN, ARNOLD
Goodwin, Knab & Company
340 West Huron
Chicago, Illinois 60610, U.S.A.
Tel: (312) 337-2010

GOTTSCHALK & ASH
INTERNATIONAL
11 Bishop Street
Toronto, Ontario, Canada
M5R 1N3
Tel: (416) 963-9717

GRAFIK COMMUNICATIONS,
LTD.
300 Montgomery Street
Alexandria, Virginia 22314, U.S.A.
Tel: (703) 683-4686

GRANT TANDY LTD.
365 Bloor Street East, 18th Floor
Toronto, Ontario, Canada
M4W 3L4
Tel: (416) 968-0201

HELMKEN,
CHARLES MICHAEL
Vice President
Council for Advancement &
Support of Education
11 Dupont Circle, Suite 400
Washington, DC 20036, U.S.A.
Tel: (202) 328-5911

HODGSON, BARBARA
Art Director
Douglas & McIntyre
1615 Venables
Vancouver, British Columbia,
Canada
V6R 3R3
Tel: (604) 254-7191

HORNALL ANDERSON
DESIGN WORKS
411 1st Avenue South, Suite 710
Seattle, Washington 98104, U.S.A.
Tel: (206) 467-5800

HUEBNER KILVERT INC.
P.O. Box 305
Cultus Lake, British Columbia,
Canada
V0X 1H0
Tel: (604) 858-6427

ROBERT HYLAND
DESIGN & ASSOCIATES
44 Laird Drive
Toronto, Ontario, Canada
M4G 3T2
Tel: (416) 424-4975

IRELAND, JIM
C.B. Media
70 The Esplanade, 2nd Floor
Toronto, Ontario, Canada
M5E 1R2
Tel: (416) 364-4266

JOHNS, DAVID
President
David Johns & Associates
130 Oriole Parkway, Suite 107
Toronto, Ontario, Canada
M5P 2G8
Tel: (416) 484-9768

KAY, GEORGE
Ann Ames Design Associates Inc.
1110 Yonge Street
Toronto, Ontario, Canada
M4W 2L6
Tel: (416) 928-3282

KUNZ, ANITA
230 Ontario Street
Toronto, Ontario, Canada
M5A 2V5
Tel: (416) 364-3846

MARTIN, MARYETTA
Martin/Maryetta Incorporated
285 Waverley Road
Toronto, Ontario, Canada
M4L 3T5
Tel: (416) 690-0055

MAYRS, FRANK
121 Basswood Lane
Aylmer East, Quebec, Canada
J9H 5E1
Tel: (819) 827-0201

MEDINA, FERNANDO
Medina Design
3007 Sherbrooke West
Montreal, Quebec, Canada
H3Z 2X8
Tel: (514) 935-8092

MÉTZ, FRÉDERIC
Université du Quebec à Montréal
C.P. 8888, Succ. A
Montreal, Quebec, Canada
H3C 3P8
Tel: (514) 282-3921

PILON, ALAIN
Université du Québec à Montréal
C.P. 8888, Succ. A
Montreal, Quebec, Canada
H3C 3P8
Tel: (514) 282-3921

ROCH, ERNST
Roch Design
P.O. Box 1056, Station B
Montreal, Quebec, Canada
H3B 3K5
Tel: (514) 866-2689

SEAGER, DAVID M.
Art Director
National Geographic Society
17th & M Streets, N.W.
Washington, DC 20036, U.S.A.
Tel: (202) 857-7538

SMITH, NEVILLE
Graphic Designer
Neville Smith Graphic Design
131 Mayburry, Skyridge
Aylmer, Quebec, Canada
J9H 5E1
Tel: (819) 827-1832

SMITH, RON BAXTER
39 Parliament Street
Toronto, Ontario, Canada
M5A 2Y2
Tel: (416) 365-1429

TAYLOR & BROWNING
DESIGN ASSOCIATES
10 Price Street
Toronto, Ontario, Canada
M4W 1Z4
Tel: (416) 927-7094

TELMET DESIGN ASSOCIATES
553 Queen Street West, #300
Toronto, Ontario, Canada
M5V 2B6
Tel: (416) 366-5646

TERRY O COMMUNICATIONS
INC.
195 Church Street
Toronto, Ontario, Canada
M5B 1Y7
Tel: (416) 864-0488

WELLER, DON
The Weller Institute for the
Cure of Design, Inc.
P.O. Box 726
Park City, Utah 84060, U.S.A.
Tel: (801) 649-9859

WOOLEY, BARBARA
Saturday Night Group
511 King Street West, Suite 100
Toronto, Ontario, Canada
M5V 2Z4
Tel: (416) 591-8822

PHOTOGRAPHY
DIRECTORY

BARABAN, JOE
President
Joe Baraban Photography
2426 Bartlett #2
Houston, Texas 77098, U.S.A.
Tel: (713) 526-0317

SMITH, RON BAXTER
39 Parliament Street
Unit 4
Toronto, Ontario, Canada
M5A 2Y2
Tel: (416) 365-1429

BENDER & BENDER
PHOTOGRAPHY
281 Klingel Road
Box 201
Waldo, Ohio 43356, U.S.A.
Tel: (614) 726-2470

CAMPBELL-SMITH, STRUAN
Struan Photographic Inc.
4 New Street
Toronto, Ontario, Canada
M5R 1P6
Tel: (416) 923-9311

CHRISTOPHER, PETER
P.O. Box 5820
Station A
Toronto, Ontario, Canada
M5W 1T2
Tel: (416) 928-9080

THE DAVIDSON BENARD
GROUP
390 Dupont Street
Suite 202
Toronto, Ontario, Canada
M5R 1V9
Tel: (416) 922-5212

DIMSON, THEO
President
Theo Dimson Design Inc.
96 Avenue Road
Toronto, Ontario, Canada
M5R 2H3
Tel: (416) 923-2427

DOJC, YURI
President
Yuri Dojc Inc.
66 Portland Street
Toronto, Ontario, Canada
M5V 2M8
Tel: (416) 366-8081

DUKA, LONNIE
Lonnie Duka Photography
919 Oriole Drive
Laguna Beach, California 92651,
U.S.A.
Tel: (714) 494-7057

DUNBAR, GEORGE
IBM Canada Ltd.
3500 Steeles Avenue East
Markham, Ontario, Canada
L3R 2Z1
Tel: (416) 474-2073

ERRICO, SAM
Errico Photography
13811 W. Capitol Drive
#119
Brookfield, WI 53005, U.S.A.
Tel: (414) 541-9182

FROOMER, BRETT
39 East 12 Street
Studio #203
New York, New York 10003, U.S.A.
Tel: (212) 533-3113

FURMAN GRAPHIC DESIGN
400 Slater
Suite 1902
Ottawa, Ontario, Canada
K1R 7S7
Tel: (613) 230-1384

KAN, GARRY
Bay 7, 4220-23rd Street N.E.
Calgary, Alberta, Canada
T2E 6X7
Tel: (403) 250-6882

KAPLAN, CAROL
20 Beacon Street
Boston, MA 02108, U.S.A.
Tel: (617) 720-4400

KOHN, MICHAEL
Oyster Studio
67 Mowat Ave., #332
Toronto, Ontario, Canada
M6K 3E3
Tel: (416) 588-1889

LEVINE, RON
Ron Levine Photography
1511 St. Jacques St. W.
Montreal, Quebec, Canada
H3C 1H4
Tel: (514) 932-8069

LLEWELLYN, ROBERT
P.O. Drawer L.
Charlottesville, VA 22903, U.S.A.
Tel: (804) 973-8000

MONTREAL CE MOIS-CI
Les Magazines Montreal Inc.
1844 William Street
2nd Floor
Montreal, Quebec, Canada
H3J 1R5
Tel: (514) 937-5771

MASON MORFIT, INC.
897 Independence Ave., 5-D
Mountain View, California 94043,
U.S.A.
Tel: (415) 969-2209

ROGERS, CHUCK
Rogers & Bigit
1226 Spring St.
Atlanta, GA 30309, U.S.A.
Tel: (404) 872-0062

ROGOVIN, MILTON
c/o University of Washington Press
4045 Brooklyn Ave. N.E.
Seattle, Washington 98117, U.S.A.
Tel: (206) 543-4050

ROSTRON, PHILIP
Instil Productions Inc.
489 Wellington St. West
Toronto, Ontario, Canada
M5V 1E9
Tel: (416) 596-6587

ST. JOHN, RICHARD
President
The St. John Group
132 Jarvis Street
Toronto, Ontario, Canada
M5B 2B5
Tel: (416) 364-3884

SHARP, IVOR
Ivor Sharp Inc.
80 Front Street East
Toronto, Ontario, Canada
M5E 1T4
Tel: (416) 363-3991

SZURKOWSKI, LES
124 Fox Run
Barrie, Ontario, Canada
L4N 5R1
Tel: (705) 726-4521

TOMALTY, MARK
Larry Williams & Associates
449 St. Pierre
Montreal, Quebec, Canada
H2Y 2M8
Tel: (514) 849-0260

VICKERS, CAMILLE
Vickers Photography
200 W. 79 PHA
New York, New York 10024, U.S.A.
Tel: (212) 580-8649

WELLS, CRAIG
Craig Wells Photography
537 West Granada
Phoenix, Arizona 85003, U.S.A.
Tel: (602) 252-8166

WILEY, MATTHEW
Matthew Wiley Photography
483 Eastern Ave.
Toronto, Ontario, Canada
M4M 1C2
Tel: (416) 462-0112

WILLIAMS, LARRY
Larry Williams & Associates
449 St. Pierre
Montreal, Quebec, Canada
H2Y 2M8
Tel: (514) 849-1668

ILLUSTRATION
DIRECTORY

BIRTA, VICTORIA
85 Thorncliffe Park Drive
Apt. 3407
Toronto, Ontario, Canada
M4H 1H0
Tel: (416) 421-7251

CHAFE-MOOTE, JANE
565 Sherbourne Street, #312
Toronto, Ontario, Canada
M4X 1W7
Tel: (416) 968-1924

CISS, JULIUS
Julius Ciss Illustration Inc.
73 Pauline Avenue
Toronto, Ontario, Canada
M6H 3M7
Tel: (416) 534-5268

CONGE, BOB
Conge Design
28 Harper Street
Rochester, New York 14607, U.S.A.
Tel: (716) 473-0291

COUSINEAU, NORMAND
Les Éditions Vice Versa
400 McGill
Montreal, Quebec, Canada
H2Y 2G1
Tel: (514) 849-0042

DAIGLE, STÉPHAN
Les Éditions Vice Versa
400 McGill
Montreal, Quebec, Canada
H2Y 2G1
Tel: (514) 849-0042

DALLISON, KEN
Pen & Ink Enterprises Ltd.
R.R. #3
Indian River, Ontario, Canada
K0L 2B0
Tel: (705) 295-4351

DAVIS, BILL
2058 Coleman Court
Simi, California 93063, U.S.A.
Tel: (805) 526-5128

INDUSTRIAL MANAGEMENT
Clifford/Elliot Limited
Royal Life Building
277 Lakeshore Road East
Box 247
Oakville, Ontario, Canada
L6J 6L9
Tel: (416) 842-2884

DOBBS, LINDA KOOLURIS
50 Prince Arthur Ave., #601
Toronto, Ontario, Canada
M5R 1B5
Tel: (416) 960-8984

FRASER, JOHN
John Fraser Studio
379 Adelaide Street West
Suite 404
Toronto, Ontario, Canada
M5V 1S5
Tel: (416) 368-2559

GLENBOW MUSEUM
130 - 9 Avenue S.E.
Calgary, Alberta, Canada
T2G 0P3
Tel: (403) 264-8300

HEINE, MARK
Total Graphics
1607 W. 2nd
Vancouver, British Columbia,
Canada
V6J 1H3
Tel: (604) 688-2862

HOLT, RINEHART AND
WINSTON OF CANADA
55 Horner Ave.
Toronto, Ontario, Canada
M8Z 4X6
Tel: (416) 255-4491

INTERISANO, MICHAEL
Michael Interisano Photography
252 Rundlefield Road N.E.
Calgary, Alberta, Canada
T1Y 2W1
Tel: (403) 234-5564

KRITCHMAN-KNUTESON,
JOAN
Advertising Art Studios, Inc.
710 N. Plankinton Ave., #800
Milwaukee, Wisconsin 53203-2454,
U.S.A.
Tel: (414) 276-6306

LEMIEUX, MICHELE
5155 de Bordeaux
Montreal, Quebec, Canada
H2H 2A6
Tel: (514) 525-6594

LEVERT, MIREILLE
5187 Jeanne Mance #3
Montreal, Quebec, Canada
H2V 4K2
Tel: (514) 273-8329

MARTIN, DOUG
Martin/Maryetta Incorporated
285 Waverley Road
Toronto, Ontario, Canada
M4L 3T5
Tel: (416) 690-0055

MCNEELY, TOM
63A Yorkville Avenue
Toronto, Ontario, Canada
M5R 1B7
Tel: (416) 925-1929

MEDINA, FERNANDO
Medina Design
3007 Sherbrooke West
Montreal, Quebec, Canada
H3Z 2X8
Tel: (514) 935-8092

MONTREAL CE MOIS-CI
Les Magazines Montreal Inc.
1844 William Street
2nd Floor
Montreal, Quebec, Canada
H3J 1R5
Tel: (514) 937-5771

MONTREAL MAGAZINE
Les Magazines Montreal Inc.
1844 William Street
2nd Floor
Montreal, Quebec, Canada
H3J 1R5
Tel: (514) 937-5771

MORGAN, LEONARD E.
President
Leonard E. Morgan Inc..
131 Ridgewood Court
Bolingbrook, Illinois 60439, U.S.A.
Tel: (312) 759-3987

OLBINSKI, J. RAFAL
Papermania Studio
111-39 76 Road, #E1
Forest Hills, New York 11375,
U.S.A.
Tel: (718) 793-7116

REID, BARBARA
Noodle Studio
70 Charles St. E.
Suite 11
Toronto, Ontario, Canada
M4Y 1T1
Tel: (416) 929-0637

SCHARF, LINDA
Scharf Illustration
45 Dwight Street
Brookline, MA 02146, U.S.A.
Tel: (617) 738-9294

SIMON, EDITH
2 Berkeley St., #601
Toronto, Ontario, Canada
M5A 2W3
Tel: (416) 369-0067

SLOAN, CLIFF
President
Sloan Art, Inc.
143 West 96th St.
New York, New York 10025, U.S.A.
Tel: (212) 977-7745

SYLVESTRE, DANIEL
Les Editions Vice Versa
400 McGill
Montreal, Quebec, Canada
H2Y 2G1
Tel: (514) 849-0042

TUGHAN, JAMES
1179A King St. W.
Suite 310
Toronto, Ontario, Canada
M6K 3C5
Tel: (416) 535-9149

TUNDRA BOOKS INC.
1434 Ste.-Catherine St. W.
#308
Montreal, Quebec, Canada
H3G 1R4
Tel: (514) 932-5434

VERBOOM, KLAAS
c/o Sandy Snelgrove Gallery
363 Talbot Street
London, Ontario, Canada
M6A 2R5
Tel: (519) 672-5225

YAMADA, TADAMI
11-9 Kami Soshigaya 5-chome
Setagaya-ku, Tokyo, Japan 157
Tel: (03) 300-2942

PRINTING
DIRECTORY

ADAMS ENGRAVING LIMITED
S. Diane Denman
73 Railside Road, Unit 7
Don Mills, Ontario, Canada
M3A 1B2
Tel: (416) 446-1382

ARTHURS-JONES
LITHOGRAPHING LTD.
1060 Tristar Drive
Mississauga, Ontario, Canada
L5T 1H9
Tel: (416) 673-0700

M.C. CHARTERS & CO. LTD.
535 Queen Street East
Toronto, Ontario, Canada
M4G 3T2
Tel: (416) 366-2788

GAYLORD CORPORATE
39 Stoffel Drive
Rexdale, Ontario, Canada
M9W 1B1
Tel: (416) 245-5252

MACLEAN HUNTER PRINTING
4601 Yonge Street
Willowdale, Ontario, Canada
M2N 5L9
Tel: (416) 221-1131

PAPERWORKS PRESS LIMITED
2943 19 St. N.E.
Calgary, Alberta, Canada
T2E 7A2
Tel: (403) 250-1264

PROVINCIAL GRAPHICS INC.
395 Steelcase Road East
Markham, Ontario, Canada
L3R 1G3
Tel: (416) 475-9150

SAMCO PRINTERS LTD.
541 Howe Street
Vancouver, British Columbia,
Canada
V6C 2C2
Tel: (604) 683-6991